CRE▲TIVE
HOMEOWNER®

Dream Log Homes & Plans

CREATIVE HOMEOWNER,® Upper Saddle River, New Jersey

DREAM LOG HOMES & PLANS

SENIOR EDITOR	Kathie Robitz
GRAPHIC DESIGNER	Kathryn Wityk
PHOTO EDITOR	Stan Sudol
PHOTO COORDINATOR	Robyn Poplasky
JUNIOR EDITOR	Jennifer Calvert
EDITORIAL ASSISTANT	Nora Grace
DIGITAL IMAGING SPECIALIST	Frank Dyer
INDEXER	Schroeder Indexing Services
COVER DESIGN	Kathryn Wityk
FRONT PHOTOGRAPHY	Roger Wade
BACK COVER PHOTOGRAPHY	(left) Courtesy of Rocky Mountain Log Homes; (right, both) Roger Wade

CREATIVE HOMEOWNER

VICE PRESIDENT AND PUBLISHER	Timothy O. Bakke
PRODUCTION DIRECTOR	Kimberly H. Vivas
ART DIRECTOR	David Geer
MANAGING EDITOR	Fran J. Donegan

Current Printing (last digit)
10 9 8 7 6 5 4 3 2 1

Dream Log Homes & Plans, First Edition
Library of Congress Control Number: 2007935569
ISBN-10: 1-58011-400-8
ISBN-13: 978-1-58011-400-4
CREATIVE HOMEOWNER®
A Division of Federal Marketing Corp.
24 Park Way
Upper Saddle River, NJ 07458
www.creativehomeowner.com

Dedication

To my parents, Mary and Leo Giromini,
for their encouragement and love.

Acknowledgments

Many thanks to all of the homeowners and manufacturers who generously
offered their time and assistance. I also want to express my gratitude to
the staff at Creative Homeowner, particularly Kathie Robitz and Kathryn Wityk,
and the team who brought this book to life. I especially wish to thank my
partner Miriam Hernández for her help and support throughout this project.

Contents

Introduction

 t a time when mass-produced "cookie cutter" houses alter the residential landscape, the log home has recaptured the attention of people who are looking for something a little different and yet traditional. Whether it's a lakeside cabin, a mountain retreat, or a suburban residence, today's log homes are as diverse as the people who own them, appealing to those who are passionate about distinctive architecture and love the natural beauty and warmth of wood. If you're thinking of building a log home—be it custom or constructed from a kit—*Dream Log Homes & Plans* can help you plan the project and provide a range of design options and ideas that will inspire you.

Today's handcrafted log home is the perfect mix of rustic materials and modern technology—designed to appeal to homeowners who want to combine contemporary living and a traditional spirit.

The Big Picture

Selecting the right log home comes with a checklist of many things to consider—the location, budget, size, the variety of log species, and corner cuts. *Deam Log Homes & Plans* guides you through this process. Subsequent chapters will take you on a tour of various types of kitchens, bedrooms, baths, and entire homes, featuring in-depth interviews with owners, designers, and builders of these uniquely styled dwellings. You'll see how the comfortable familiarity of a log-home interior can make the coming together of family and friends extra special. Decorating challenges dictated by the size, shape, and color of the logs will be explored. *Dream Log Homes & Plans* also examines the options and satisfaction of choosing the right furnishings.

LEFT: The comfortable, laid-back ambiance of a log home creates a warm atmosphere for the gathering of family and friends, making it an ideal choice for those who prefer a carefree lifestyle.

ABOVE: With its massive stone fireplace and private patio, this master bedroom is the perfect retreat. French doors and windows provide a view of the lake and fill the bedroom with natural sunlight.

RIGHT: Choosing natural materials, such as the stone and treated-wood paneling in this bathroom, enhances the craftsmanship that is intrinsic in a log home.

More Than Style Ideas

But interior design is only part of the story. *Dream Log Homes & Plans* goes beyond the inside of the house to feature an abundant variety of designs for decks, patios, and porches. The fact that nature plays such an integral part of log-home living allows these outdoor rooms to be used for expanding the space and, in many cases, year-round enjoyment.

Maintenance of a log house is quite different from that of a vinyl-clad home with a composite deck, and the final chapter will show you steps to take to protect your home from insects, weather, and general wear and tear. There are also tips for maintaining interior log surfaces.

Dream Log Homes & Plans is a book about the challenges and the many design options for building a log home. The ideas throughout this book provide suggestions and inspiration, awakening your imagination to the vast possibilities of log-cabin living. If your interest is heightened, there are log-home plans you can purchase, starting on page 194.

Building a
Log Home

nce the favorite abode of frontiersmen and frontierswomen, the log cabin has come a long way in the annals of architecture. Today's designs range from charming cozy cottages to sophisticated mansions. Advanced construction techniques, modern joinery systems, and technologically advanced materials have made the modern log home appealing to a large section of the population. Whether you are planning to build a log home or just dreaming about the possibility, having the correct information and expert advice at hand will make the experience an exciting and fulfilling one.

Cabin or Luxury Home?

Where do you begin? Factors such as size, whether you are planning a small getaway cabin in the woods or a spacious full-time dwelling, will play a large part in your final decision. It's not the dimensions but the quality of the workmanship that is important. With careful planning you can live very comfortably in a small 1,200-square-foot cabin. On the other hand, if you are planning to live in the house full-time now or plan to move in when you retire, you'll have to reconsider the size. One of the worst mistakes you can make is designing a home that is not big enough or, conversely, that it is more than you need.

Whatever you decide, you have probably spent some time combing through books and magazines filled with appealing photos and interesting floor plans. Doing this is only part of your homework. You are also going to have to take stock of the big picture. That includes choosing a location, working out a budget, and deciding on a style. Start planning by becoming familiar with the many material options available, from the type and species of log to roofing materials and weather proofing. This knowledge will save you both time and money when it comes time to sit down with the professionals.

While committing to building a log home can be intimidating, it is best to remain objective. To prevent yourself from becoming overwhelmed, don't think about everything at once. Slow it down; break it

This rustic weekend cabin, perched on the edge of a cliff, features a wraparound covered porch designed to take advantage of the spectacular bird's-eye view of the nearby mountain range.

Classic peaked rooflines, a standard design component in many log homes, are used here in multiples to create a striking first impression. Even the structural elements, such as support beams, are designed to be aesthetically pleasing.

down; and write it down. Itemize all of the things you would want your new home to be; then start to gather all of the information you can.

Get Organized

Compile a checklist of the things you must have, plus a wish list of things you dream of having. This list will come in handy when you work out your budget. It will remind you to put first things first and prevent you from purchasing budget-busters that you may want but don't really need.

Keep all of your data together by using loose-leaf binders to hold your various photos and clippings. When you're collecting photos, make a note about the sources.

OPPOSITE: In log-home construction, a simple element such as bleached wood can make a dramatic statement. Here the light tone of the logs brings out the clean lines of the building's design, while highlighting the front door.

ABOVE: Weather plays an important part in choosing building materials for your log home. Keep in mind that if you build in an area that gets snow, you'll have to select a roof that will support the extra weight.

Separate the binders into sections for photos or sketches of rooms, exteriors, and landscaping ideas. Include a list of the various professionals you will need on your team and, whenever possible, what things will cost. If you come across a house that you like, write or visit the manufacturer's Web site and ask if you can get a floor plan. Many companies also offer DVDs, CDs, videos, and catalogs that showcase floor plans and pricing.

Start a collection of magazines devoted to log homes. These publications are a wonderful source of reference materials. Most of the magazines will contain listings of recent log-home shows taking place in your area. These expos are packed with the latest information about log-home building, featuring everything from seminars to free samples. Expos also offer the future log-home owner the chance to meet local professionals face to face. You'll also find yourself hobnobbing with seasoned log-home owners who can pass on valuable advice. Before you go, make sure you have your lists with you, and be prepared to ask questions of the producers.

Another great source of information is manufacturers' model homes. Check the log-home producers in your area regarding open houses. Model homes are not only an excellent way to see actual log buildings in person but provide an opportunity to talk one-on-one with a manufacturer's representative. Visiting log homes will give you a better chance to view all of your options, including the size of the home where you would be comfortable, who will be involved in the work, and how much your money will buy.

Location, Location, Location

One of the first things to consider before you start planning your log home is the location of the building site. Because there are always variations in any terrain, it is best to know what you will be facing geographically before you design your home. Talk to a general contractor about development costs before you invest in untamed acreage. Keep in mind the placement and orientation of the house in order to take full advantage of the views and natural light. You might also want to consider

working with a land developer who sells parcels of land to individual buyers. Some of these developers sell their properties exclusively as part of a log-home community. An added advantage is the fact that the land comes already equipped with utilities, road access, and in many cases, maintenance and landscaping services.

In addition to the terrain, inclement weather will also play a big part in the type of materials you choose for your log home. Some communities may mandate special structural requirements to assure the home will stand up against harsh weather or natural disasters. Check with your local building-code authority and ask about the design requirements for obtaining a building permit.

If you build on a mountain in a cold climate, plan for lots of snow. This means that the roof will have to support extra weight. The standard roof load for snow country is 125 pounds per square foot.

Heating

The thermal property of logs gives them the ability to absorb and release heat. Once the logs warm up they stay that way over a period of time. One of the most popular ways to heat new log homes is radiant, in-floor heating. Pleasant, clean, and easy to install, radiant heat warms a home silently and invisibly and can be used under most flooring, including wood. Radiant heat will initially cost more, but the lower operating costs over the years will more than pay for itself. "Radiant heat on the main floor is a great choice because this is the coolest part of the house," says Glen Hyman, Owner/Designer, Great House Design, Washington State. "I also recommend secondary units on the upper floors such as strip heaters that work with water, not electricity. Most homeowners want to romanticize the heating of their home with a fireplace. This is fine for aesthetic reasons but not for heating. A fireplace can suck the

OPPOSITE: Oversize windows overlooking a large deck define the rear elevation of this log mountain home. The placement and orientation of a house should always take advantage of the views and direction of natural light.

LEFT: The half-sawn logs used for interior walls create a smooth, flat finish that contrasts with the room's solid-pine posts and beams. A trio of large windows opens the space to woodland views.

heat right out of a house. A better solution is a wood-burning stove—freestanding or inserted in the fireplace, or a pellet stove."

To prevent ice buildup that can cause damage, cold environments also require insulated roofs with venting systems to pull cold air into the eves and exhaust warm air through the ridge of the roof.

A Unique Style

The size of your finished home will affect the number of logs needed, the amount of labor involved, as well as the quantity of materials necessary for structural integrity. Shape, color, size, and texture of the logs will also have an impact on the style of the home. Will the design include dormers, a dramatic roofline, or a spectacular deck? All of these factors will affect the overall cost of the finished home. The estimated log portion of a home usually accounts for 20–50 percent of the home's finished cost. This is based on the wide range in log options. Full-log construction using 12-inch logs will be more expensive than 6 x 8-inch logs. Smaller logs are readily available making the price more competitive.

Log Profiles

A producer can mill your logs any way you want, but you will save time and money if you go with a traditional profile. Rectangular and square logs have more of an Early American look. Combined with

ABOVE: This interior wall incorporates three-sided, D-shape notched logs that are designed to include structural log ends in the room's architecture. Interior log ends can provide visual interest to any area of a room.

OPPOSITE: Log architecture can be successfully mixed with a variety of natural materials, such as slate, stone, and metal. This home reflects a medieval style that was popular with many early European settlers.

rough finishes and chinking, the look can be that of an old building that has been standing for two or three hundred years. Manufacturers have been able to develop a machine that mimics a handmade look or will use draw knives on the logs after they have been milled to give the appearance of hand-hewing without the expense. These logs are more expensive than standard milled logs but cheaper than ones that are made by hand.

The Right Angle

A big difference between a standard framed house and a log cabin is the way the interior corners intersect. Because of the precise fitting required, log corners are the most-expensive part of your wall systems. Keeping the corners at 90 degrees will save money on labor costs. If you are planning a bump-out window to catch a glorious view, consider going with a rectangle instead of a bow shape. Reduce the number of corners in your home whenever possible. If your design contains interesting, but costly, corners and conversation areas framed by protruding logs, try to eliminate the corners and use interior design, rugs, furniture groupings, and low bookcases to create smaller areas within the room.

In some cases, you will have a vertical stack of log ends protruding into the room. Log ends can project anywhere into a room depending on the layout and plan. Taking this into consideration will help you accommodate where you want to place

OPPOSITE: Hand-hewn logs, timber framing, and pine paneling create an expansive framework for this open great room. Coated with a nearly transparent finish, the white-pine interior has a bright, fresh look.

BELOW: Shape, texture, and color of the wood are important factors in determining the character and style of a building. Here, round logs are flattened on top and bottom, allowing the pieces to fit snugly on top of one another.

your furniture. Most log-home owners actually like the look of log ends and plan their furniture arrangements accordingly.

Dovetail joinery is another option. Make sure you hire an experienced craftsperson—dovetailing has to be carefully fitted in each corner of the structure, interlocking the connecting walls to one another. It takes years of experience to accomplish an exact level of joinery.

Wood is expensive and log homes are very labor intensive to build. This is why getting the right help is so important. Designing a log home requires specialized skills and knowledge. There are certain planning and decorative choices that are unique to log homes. For example, the number of framed walls, cabinetry, stairways, and partitions can add extra expense to your overall budget because they all will have to be carefully scribed into the logs to ensure a tight fit.

Money Matters

First things first: knowing how much money you can afford to spend on your new home is a crucial part of the planning process. When using a lender to obtain a mortgage, a homeowner will often budget a specific amount toward a project and expect the lender to automatically approve the amount. Unfortunately, that doesn't always work. Most lenders use a formula based on your monthly income and ongoing expenses to determine the loan payment you can afford. For more information, check your lender's Web site or BankRate.com, and enter your own numbers into their "Borrower Qualifying Calculator."

Start with your existing lender to see if they will finance your new home. If not, look into owner-builder construction loans or any of the log-home lending specialists listed on the Internet or yellow pages.

Because these lenders are accustomed to working with people who are building log homes, they are often able to offer competitive rates and may even help you find qualified builders and manufacturers in your area.

When you are planning your budget you'll need to factor in the cost of the land, site-prep work, foundation, masonry, plumbing and heating supplies, insulation, countertops, kitchen cabinets, finished flooring, sealants, and other interior and exterior finishes. The amount will also be based on the quality of items you choose. High-end appliances and kitchen cabinets can easily run up the cost by 50 percent or more. Leave a little extra for unexpected expenses that are bound to surface during construction. If your initial budget takes your breath away, calmly sit down and ask yourself what you can do without that might make your budget manageable. If this seems like a lot of work, remember that it will save you from major headaches in the future.

Find out your lender's preapproval process. There will be specific requirements that must be met before they will issue a letter guaranteeing the amount they are willing to loan you. Working with a mortgage lender to get pre-approved before you start will free you to concentrate on the fun part: planning your dream home. Before you apply for a mortgage, check your credit report online or by phone for any potential snags or incorrect information. If you have any credit problems, be sure to discuss them with the mortgage brokers to find out how to repair the situation.

LEFT: Many manufactures offer full or partial log-home kits that range from a complete turnkey home to a log-shell package that includes exterior elements from the foundation to the rafters.

OPPOSITE: A soaring 25-ft. cathedral ceiling is accented with full-log rafters and a grand stairway with decorative log railing. The loft area above provides a visual separation for the room below it.

Custom Built or Manufactured?

There is no such thing as a simple log cabin; even a small one requires precision craftsmanship. Fortunately, there is a wide choice of building methods, both custom and manufactured.

Manufactured homes use machine-peeled and notched logs that are precision cut. Because each piece is a clean cut, the manufacturer can piece together short logs to span a wall with barely discernable seams. The overall appearance will be more uniform and consistent. Manufacturers of machine-milled logs usually work with shorter, smaller trees that are readily available and affordable. The milled logs are then assembled before shipment in order to make sure everything fits precisely. Many log-home manufacturers further simplify the building process by offering full or partial packages known as "kits." These pack-

ages provide the homeowner with all of the basic materials needed to build a house. In some cases, you can purchase a log-shell package that only provides the exterior parameters of the house from foundation to roofline minus the windows and doors. You would then either purchase a separate door-and-window package from the manufacturer or buy these items through local suppliers. This gives you the opportunity to create a semicustom home without the challenge of starting from scratch.

A full log-home package might include doors, windows, flooring, rafters, and roofing materials. Plumbing, wiring, and HVAC are rarely, if ever, part of a kit.

Although manufactured homes can save you money, there are many factors that will raise the price of even the most basic design. One of these is the choice of wood. For example, pine is a lot less expensive than walnut. Another price adjuster is poor planning that requires change orders, resulting in extra labor costs.

Handcrafted log homes start off as individual trees that are peeled or hand-hewn and carefully fitted together using special techniques and tools. These custom log homes use large-diameter trees with longer straight trunks, some of which will extend the entire length of the wall without splicing. The overall look is more rustic than milled logs. In contrast to manufactured log-home kits, handcrafters usually limit their business to fabricating the structure of the house. If you choose a handcrafted

home you will have to rely on your contractor to obtain the extras—doors, windows, flooring, and framing lumber.

Unlike milled-wood companies, handcrafters do not employ designers but will, on occasion, refer clients to architects. After the construction drawings are prepared, the handcrafter will obtain the logs and fabricate the building in their yard. They then tag and number each piece, disassemble the house, and transport it to your site. It's the time and labor involved that makes a handcrafted structure typically more expensive than a machine-milled log house.

Choosing A Log-Home Builder

Before you decide on a builder, try to have a clear idea of the style home you want. There is such a wide choice of styles from which to choose, including the size, shape, and color of the logs and the type of corner and roofing system. Knowing what you want beforehand will save a lot of time. After you have defined the style of home you want, pick out several log-building companies that match your interest. Then comparison shop. Most log-home manufacturers have competent craftsmen on staff, as well as a working relationship with various contractors around the country. Some log companies even have in-house architects and designers who can work with you to create your plans. Find out what their policy is about initial consulting, drawing up preliminary plans, changing plans, and other services.

In some cases, builder services can include recommending qualified subcontractors and lending institutions that work with log-home financing.

SMART IDEA

Take your time shopping for the right location before you commit to building your log home. Some homeowners have purchased land a year or more before building. Finding the perfect site will make it easier to plan the perfect home.

OPPOSITE: Many log-home manufacturers have skilled craftsmen and builders on their staff, as well as working relationships with independent contractors around the country who specialize in log-home construction.

LEFT: Log-home manufacturers also offer plans for various types of decorative outbuildings, such as this gazebo, designed to complement the main house and expand the outdoor-living space.

This front-hall stairway features half-log treads with handcrafted log railings. Some manufacturers allow adjustments to their log packages, such as custom-designed stairs. These changes can add a unique look to a room but will also have an impact on the bottom line.

OPPOSITE: Buying a log-shell package may only provide you with an exterior framework. You may need to purchase the windows, exterior doors, and a roof-and-rafters package separately.

Make sure you also understand the standard systems and the options that are available. Roofing systems can have the basic design, which consists of *dimensional-lumber rafters* similar to a roof found in a conventional home. This type of roof is the least expensive but lacks the exposed logs or timbers associated with log homes. Another system is the *exposed rafter*, made up of a timber or log framework covered with lumber, insulation, and the exterior roof covering. Most providers offer a choice of several roof systems. "*Metal roofing* is my favorite choice for log homes," says Bob Marcom, Director of Sales, Strongwood Log Homes, Mt. Juliet, Tennessee. "It's a very practical material for areas of heavy snowfall. The snow will usually just slide right off. Metal roofs are lightweight, fireproof, and come in a wide variety of styles and colors. The only drawback is the cost, which can run around two to three times more than standard asphalt shingle."

Other factors to think about are the combinations of logs and corner styles that are offered today. Many builders use whole round logs; some will hew the logs flat on two, three, or four sides. Certain companies use handcrafted logs; others use machines to shape, cope, and notch the logs.

The amount of time, expertise, and labor that goes into handcrafted log homes makes them more expensive than homes built with machine-milled logs. Costs can also depend on the log wood species you request. Most log manufacturers prefer a particular species they are familiar with and work with most often, but are usually open to other options. Selection preference usually includes texture, density, color, and

strength. Tim Bullock of Bullock and Company, Ontario, Canada, likes eastern white pine. " I think it's the prettiest, readily available, and renewable wood in our area," he says. Builders can help you decide on a species that works within your needs and your budget. If you prefer a species from another area that is far from home, be prepared to spend more money on the transportation. Don't base your cost on the price of raw logs. The final cost may include the unexpected expense of debarking, pressure washing, and the treating and drying of logs.

Every new house built with wood will settle over time. In the case of a frame house, it could be a fraction of an inch, for kiln-dried milled logs, it could be a little more. Logs will actually shrink depending on the moisture content of the wood; "dried" logs have lost most of their moisture and shrink less than "green" logs. In a hand-hewn, round-log house, the shrinkage

SMART IDEA

Be sure to ask each manufacturer the following questions:
- How long have you been in business?
- What wood species do you use?
- What drying method do you use?
- How will the logs arrive at my site?
- What exactly will the package contain?
- Are the doors, windows, roofing, and other materials offered in the package brand names I would recognize?
- What type of log profile do you provide?
- Do you offer various corner styles?
- What type of warranty do you offer?

Be sure to discuss your budget and the professionals' fees up front.

METAL ROOFING

Once the darling of the warehouse set, metal roofing has become the latest fashion statement in the residential housing market. Because it lasts longer than composition shingles and requires less maintenance, metal roofing has also gained a following in the log-home industry.

Although not recognized as a traditional log-home look, many builders are starting to offer this utilitarian material to their clients. Metal roofs will cost more, but can have warranties up to 20 years long. But the average life can run up to 50 years because the warranty usually applies specifically to the color. Metal roofs easily shed ice and snow in the winter and reflect the sun's heat in the summer.

can be as much as an inch or two. Settling is usually slight, but experienced log-home builders have ways to deal with it so that it does not cause problems later.

Once you've decided on several manufacturers, make sure you carefully research their business practices and change policies. Typically, the provider's package price will include preliminary plans, a set of revisions, and a final blueprint. Any changes to the final blueprint will probably cost extra. Find out how much. Carefully check your initial plan to make sure you have the floor plan you want. If not, that's the time to make changes. Should you decide to add an extra room, such as a half bath or mudroom, to the original plan, ask the manufacturer to give a quote on the cost. This is also a good time to go over everything with your contractor and recheck your budget.

Working with an Architect

If you decide to work with your own architect, be sure to find one that specializes in designing log homes. However, if this is not possible, ask your architect to work with a qualified log builder or log-building company at the beginning of the project. Manufacturers can offer different log specification, structural features, and wall connections—things an architect needs to know about before he or she starts designing. The more architects know about log buildings, the better able they are to use their creative talents to produce remarkable buildings. If you are looking for an architect familiar with the intricacies of log construction, visit Web sites for information on builders, state-by-state listings of log-home dealers, and lists of architects with log-home experience.

This handcrafted home, featuring a 25-ft.-high cathedral ceiling with a wide-open great room and loft, is reminiscent of a spectacular nineteenth-century hunting lodge.

LOG LINGO

Air-Dried Refers to logs that have been dried in the sun. Fresh-cut logs can have more than 30 percent moisture by weight. As the logs dry, they shrink. Companies dry their logs so that shrinkage is minimized before construction.

Chinking This is the filling between the logs. Originally chinking was a combination of mortar, moss, stones, grass, or mud. Today it is chemically engineered mastic. Not all log homes use chinking.

HVAC Heating, Ventilating, and Air-Conditioning system

Joinery How the logs are joined together. Milled logs have projections called "tongues" on the upper surface and corresponding "grooves" on the under surface. When the logs are stacked, they lock into a tight fit.

Kiln-Dried To speed up the drying process, some producers dry the logs in an industrial kiln or oven. This faster method can take the moisture content of the wood down to 15 percent, producing a drier, more stable log.

Profile The cross section of a milled log. Some logs have a D-shape profile and some are completely round. Common shapes are D, round, and square.

Settling As wood dries it shrinks slightly. Dried logs shrink less than "green" logs, which still have a great deal of moisture. When logs are stacked into walls and shrink, the wall will move slightly. This is known as settling.

Standing Dead Timber The trees that have died of natural causes such as drought, disease, or in some cases, have been scorched, not burned, in forest fires. The logs can be used in structures if the dead tree is still standing and structurally sound.

Gathering Spaces

 he warm, laid-back atmosphere of a log home makes it a natural welcoming place for friends and family. Whether you live in it full-time or just on weekends, a log home is the ideal choice for those who prefer casual living—and it's perfect for creating family memories in a charming setting. You may already have an idea of what your log home will look like. Now is the time to think about how your dream will fit your lifestyle.

Start by considering each room and how you need it to function. Which rooms will you use most often? What activities are important to your family? What room will be used as the center of family life? Each room should be a reflection of your personal taste, but it should also accommodate various needs and the activities that take place there. The more closely you relate the decor to your lifestyle, the more your family's personality will be part of your log home.

Space Considerations

Plan your home so that there is plenty of separation between the public areas, such as the family room or kitchen, and the personal spaces, such as the bedrooms and baths. The main public area might be a great room, combining a living and dining room with the kitchen. Or it might be the family room. Regardless of its size, the living area should have a dramatic focal point or two that sets the stage for the rest of the room. Strong visual elements may include a large stone fireplace, a magnificent staircase, or built-in cabinetry.

Whether it's one open space or distinctly separate rooms, there should be good flow. That means you should be able to move around with ease. How you plan the layout is important within each area, as well. Do you want oversize seating areas in the living room or a large table that can accommodate twelve diners? Be sure to allow room for them in your floor plan.

RIGHT: Centered between two windows, a traditional stone fireplace creates a focal point in this small living room. Horizontal chinking lines provide an interesting contrast against the vertical shape of the fireplace.

OPPOSITE: This large elk-antler chandelier was designed to fit the proportion and scale of this great room. Placed in the middle of the room, the fixture draws the eye up, emphasizing the massive stone fireplace.

The wide doorway between the living and dining rooms was designed to create a visual separation between the two areas without closing them off to each other. This openness produces a feeling of expansiveness while allowing each space to remain distinct and independent.

Stretching

After analyzing your needs you may decide that bigger is not better after all. In that case, you can keep the space cozy but not crowded by making smart choices about furnishings. Use versatile pieces that serve more than one function, such a chair in the living room that opens into a bed or a high-low coffee table that you can adjust to a comfortable height for dining when you need it. Incorporate built-in niches, bookshelves, hutches, or an area tucked under a staircase to expand storage space. If the front door of the cabin opens into the living room, situate an étagère or open-shelving unit perpendicular to the door to create the sense of a separate entry.

Principles of Design

An understanding of the basic principles of good design—harmony, rhythm, balance, scale, proportion, and emphasis—will make wise decorating decisions easier for you. Following these classic guidelines will sharpen your eye, helping you to create pleasing interiors.

Harmony is achieved in design when all of the elements relate to one another. In other words, everything coordinates within one scheme or motif. Matching styles, colors, and patterns are good examples.

Rhythm in design is the arrangement of lines or shapes to give the impression of movement. It also refers to the use of

OPPOSITE: Extending the fireplace hearth to include an extra shelf visually enlarged a corner space in this small living room. The shelf holds storage and acts as a cozy window seat.

ABOVE RIGHT: Framing the fireplace with decorative columns and two matching chairs creates a symmetrical arrangement in this contemporary log cabin. The visual focus of the room is the fireplace, and the layout and symmetrical placement complement it.

repeated patterns, which keeps interest going around to different areas of a room. The horizontal lines of log-cabin walls convey a natural rhythm in a room.

Balance in design is the arrangement of lines and shapes to produce a feeling of equilibrium. One way to do this is by combining large and small furnishings or patterns evenly throughout the space. With balance, relationships between objects or forms seem natural and comfortable to the eye. Balanced relationships between objects can be either *symmetrical* or *asymmetrical.*

Symmetry refers to the same arrangements of parts on both sides of an imagined or real center line. An example is the placement of identical candlesticks at each end of a mantel.

Asymmetry is the balance between objects of different sizes as the result of placement. For example, picture a grouping of tall slender candlesticks on one side of a mantel and a short wide vase on the other.

Scale and proportion work hand in hand. In decorating, *scale* simply refers to the size of something as it relates to the size of everything else. *Proportion* refers to the relationship of parts or objects to one another, based on size. For example, windows that look small may not be in proportion to the size of the room. Good scale is achieved when all of the parts are proportionately correct relative to each other, as well as to the whole.

Emphasis, also known as a focal point, creates a dominant feature in a room. This may be a distinctive architectural element such as a large fireplace or a window with a view. If the room does not have a focal point, you can create one with furnishings. A large bookcase on one wall or a central seating group could be the emphasis.

Furnishing a Log Home

There are many places to look for decorating inspiration. In addition to log-home model rooms, you might also want to take note of a vacation lodge, country-style bed and breakfast, or a guest cottage where you have stayed and felt at home. What do you like about it?

The nature of a log home and its location will inspire various themes, as well: Western, Country Cabin, Adirondack Lodge, Arts and Crafts, or Contemporary.

Log styles will influence your choices, too. Remember scale and proportion. Start with the room's dimensions, but look at the logs. If they are massive, you will need a few large pieces of furniture for balance, especially if the ceiling is vaulted or high.

Rough, peeled, dark-stained logs create a rustic feeling in a room. Play it up with a casual but strong western look: leather furniture, Native American accessories, animal horns, wagon wheels, wide-plank floors, and colorful Pendleton blankets.

Logs with a hand-hewn dovetail construction inspire an early frontier-settler look. Use woven cotton-check fabrics, quilts, and painted-wood cabinets. Softer than the more masculine look described above, this American country style is informal and unpretentious—think wing chairs

SMART IDEA

Be careful of too much wood. Log-home owners can get carried away finishing the floors, ceilings, kitchens, and built-ins in matching woods. This is where the concept of balance really helps. In order for the beauty of the logs to show through, they need to be contrasted with other materials.

upholstered in a carefree striped ticking, hand-hooked rugs, and baskets filled with dried flowers.

Full-round chinking logs provide the perfect background for the Adirondack-Lodge style. This look, which is also called "camp-style decorating," is rustic, as well, but it has its own distinct characteristics. Originally designed for the interiors of summer camps and lodges that were built in upstate New York during the mid-1800s, much of this furniture was, and still is, crafted by hand. It embraces nature with its hickory and birch-veneered furniture and special pieces made from the trees' stumps, whole branches, and gnarled root. The best known is the stick furniture that is characterized by branches that have been tied or nailed together.

Today, furniture pieces may also include machine-made beds, dressers, sideboards, desks, and chairs. To add authenticity, accessories could include vintage boat paddles, sleds, or birch-bark frames.

Round milled logs work well with the Arts and Crafts style, which embraces Mission, Craftsman, and architect Frank Lloyd Wright's Prairie style. Popular today, it began as an aesthetic movement in England during the late-nineteenth century as a revolt against the mass-produced machine-made products that were a result of the Industrial Revolution.

In 1880, English designer John Ruskin published his book, *Seven Lamps of Architecture*, in which he urged a return to the handcraftsmanship of an earlier time. The

result, the Arts and Crafts movement, professed a philosophy that beautiful, simple, organic objects arranged harmoniously in a home contribute to the inhabitants' well-being. This mission to promote the natural beauty and honesty of handcraftsmanship can often be found in today's log-home construction.

Ruskin aside, and despite other purists' objections, the use of machine finishing in

OPPOSITE: A combination of flat logs, wood paneling, and drywall provides an interesting contrast of textures and colors in this small cabin.

BELOW: Oversize furnishings are just the right scale for this large, open great room. The furniture shares space with a soaring 27-ft. cathedral ceiling and massive full-log rafters.

This ranch-style living room is centered on the stone fireplace. Contemporary-style furnishings take on a Western look when upholstered in soft cowhide.

the log-home industry has resulted in many creative log profiles.

Sanded whitewashed logs and three-sided sawn logs lend themselves to a contemporary look, something unheard of in a log home a few decades ago. Unlike those of traditional log homes, the interior walls have a smooth, flat appearance, allowing them to retain the natural beauty of the wood without looking too rustic.

Lighting

Log homes are cherished for their cozy woodsy look. Unfortunately, cozy and woodsy can also mean dark. Even logs that have been whitewashed will absorb more and reflect less light than conventional white walls. It will take more supplemental lighting to brighten a log-home interior than that of a similar-size standard home.

The key to good lighting is flexibility and careful planning. When you're planning lighting, think about the general illumination of the rooms as well as brightening areas for specific activities or effect. Most rooms contain at least a combination of general and task lighting, perhaps with

ABOVE: Recessed canisters dapple light onto the logs and supplement the natural light that enters this room through the small window and glass doors.

OPPOSITE: During the day, this open loft is illuminated by a bank of large windows. At night, a chandelier on a dimmer can be set to create the perfect mood for dining.

SMART IDEA

A wiring plan for your home's sound system should include the speakers in the media room. Experts say that the acoustics inside a log home can be superb, but sound waves have a tendency to bounce off the hard surfaces of logs making it difficult to control their direction. Consult an audio engineer who will be able to work around any wiring and sound issues before you start to build.

some accent and decorative lighting, too. But not all fixtures are designed to serve every lighting need, so consult an expert before making your selections.

Ideally, a lighting plan should be devised while a house is in the design stage. Adding lighting or outlets to an existing room in a log home is not an easy task when you consider the problems posed by wiring solid logs. Careful planning will save you time and money in the long run.

First, determine how much natural light will be available in each room. Depending on the orientation of the windows, a room may get lots of early-morning light (east facing); afternoon sunlight (west facing); sun all day (south facing); or no direct sunlight (north facing).

Keep in mind the function of the room and the furniture layout. This will help you decide on how many fixtures you need and where to place them.

The latest in "smart" lighting systems features centrally located computerized control panels that can be programmed to operate the lights in different rooms or zones within one space.

OPPOSITE: A floor lamp next to the sofa or an easy chair is perfect for reading. Mixed with candles and a glowing fire, it can add a warm glow to any corner of a room.

BELOW: Decorative light fixtures provide this room with task lighting. Recessed canisters add ambient light, while spotlights are used to accent the artwork in niches and shelves.

LIGHTING SYSTEMS

- Floodlights installed in the ceiling will make a modest-size room seem larger.
- Pinpoint spotlights can focus attention on objects, such as art or collectibles.
- Low-voltage halogen spotlights or pendants can illuminate a dining table, work surface, or a kitchen island.
- Recessed spotlights or track lights can be directed to highlight particular areas of a room.

SMART IDEA

Looking for a light fixture that is not your standard elk-antler chandelier or hanging wagon wheel? Consider the industrial-style pendant light—a popular choice for both rustic and contemporary cabins. Available in a wide range of metallic and baked-on enamel finishes, this utilitarian design provides a nice contrast to wood walls.

Light Fixtures

Table and floor lamps remain popular sources of light. Because lamps are decorative as well functional, they should be chosen carefully. The first thing to consider is scale. Small delicate lamps will look out of place in a room with massive furniture and high ceilings. But have fun with lamps, because there is such wide array of whimsical shapes on the market. Why not purchase several unusual ones that can also double as artwork? Take care not to use too many lamps in one room—log homes possess a lot of visual excitement already.

Wall sconces can add style to a room, but installing them in log walls can be problematic. The design of a wall sconce may not fit the round irregularity of logs. A flat mounting plate may require cutting out a portion of the wood to make it fit. But once the fixture is installed, the shade may be pushed out of position by a protruding log. Check with your designer before buying any sconce fixtures or consult with someone at your home-lighting store.

Collections

The essence of a log house—its combination of present-day handcraftsmanship and historical reference—creates a natural setting for the display of cherished collections. Whether you are interested in Western artifacts, birdhouses, antique tools, or baskets, gathering a collection can be a life-long process of discovery and pleasure.

Collectors delight in learning the history and authenticity of unique vintage items. Learning when and where objects were made and how they were used makes a collection special. Some people like to build a collection around a family heirloom or a hobby.

You may already have a collection that is waiting to be displayed in your new home. If not, you may want to start one. There are lots of places to look for individual pieces. Check out local auction houses, flea markets, and estate sales. Antique shows might deal in more costly items but they often have the most interesting things for sale. However, never buy something unless you examine it first. That moth-eaten rug might not be the bargain you thought it was. Repairing broken items may turn out to be costly or time consuming. Also, check the many paperback price guides that are published annually. Long-time collectors will tell you that the secret to collecting is to buy what you like. The exciting part is the search.

Everyone has ideas about what makes an attractive collection and how much space to devote to it. Like a home, it should say something about its owner.

Arched stone openings help break up the expansive square footage of this magnificent lodge-like home. The homeowner's collection of paintings and sculpture are artfully displayed throughout the various rooms.

SMART IDEA

When choosing colors for your furnishings, remember that dark colors absorb light and light colors reflect it. The colors you choose will help you decide on the strength and amount of light in a room. If you have a corner area or hallway that doesn't get much light, consider hanging a mirror or adding highly polished furniture to help reflect light back into the space.

Special Architectural Features

The renewed interest in log homes dates back to the 1970s, but it wasn't until the 1980s when large companies got into the act. As interest grew, architects and interior designers began to take note of the log home. Looking at it with a creative eye, many of these designers set out to break rules and experiment with new materials.

The latest log homes are constructed not only of logs but a combination of a variety of materials, such as glass, stone, metal, and stucco. Unorthodox materials can convey a regional influence within a style. For example, whitewashed logs and bleached-wood flooring coordinate with contemporary furnishings; stone or stucco, on the other hand, can enhance American Southwest ambiance.

To Chink or Not To Chink?

Other than the distinctive shapes, patterns, and textures available, there is more to a log wall than logs. There is also the matter of *chinking*—the fill between the logs. Some wall designs call for a tight and fitted look without chinking, while others feature a wide stripe-like chinking between the logs. Some chinkings are white or can be stained to match the color of the wood. Using chinking is one of the distinctive finishings that makes log homes so unique.

Designing with Drywall

Framing interior walls in drywall not only offsets the wood but also allows more design flexibility. Painted or treated with wallcovering, drywall can add color, texture, and pattern to a room while hiding wires and plumbing. Also, a wall of standard framed drywall will take up less interior space than a wall composed of logs.

Adding Wood Decoration

Many artisans work with builders and designers to create structural or aesthetic sculpted displays of rustic arches, carved posts, beams, and other designs made of twigs, roots, and branches inside a log home. The natural curves of roots and branches can introduce intriguing lines and patterns to a staircase or a fireplace mantel. Using these types of decorative carvings and natural sculpture provide a shapely contrast to the horizontal lines inherent in log walls, and in some cases, they become the focal point in a room. Although ideas can often spring up spontaneously from a found object, implementation of such designs requires the skill and careful planning of an artisan.

RIGHT: Full-round chinked logs create strong horizontal lines across the outer walls of this ranch-style living room. Inspired by Western architecture, the room features full-log beams and clerestory windows.

OPPOSITE: Today's log homes aren't always built entirely of logs. Custom designs, such as this one, can include conventional drywall and floor-to-ceiling windows and log columns.

FAR LEFT: Prized for the beauty of its age, this reclaimed wood was salvaged from nineteenth-century factory floors. Trestle bridges and maritime structures are also becoming popular flooring sources for log homes.

LEFT: Laminate flooring, also know as "faux wood," can, in certain high-traffic areas, provide the look home-owners desire along with the aspects of durability and quick cleanup.

Flooring

In addition to walls, a floor makes up a dominant area of a room and anchors all of the other elements. Whatever type you choose, always buy the best quality you can afford. An inexpensive floor will end up costing more in maintenance and wear. Besides an endless choice of colors, flooring materials also offer a wide variety of textures.

Wood

Wood is the overwhelming choice for log homes, especially in high-traffic areas. The varieties of wood flooring are vast. Cost varies widely, too, depending on the type and grade of the wood and the choice between wood strips, random planks, and inlay designs.

Strip flooring is laid down in simple straight lines of evenly spaced narrow boards placed side by side, giving the room a smooth expansive look.

Plank flooring is similar to strip, but the boards are a random mix of narrow and wide widths, sometimes installed with pegs to achieve a more rustic look. Wood-flooring manufacturers offer a less-expensive method of machine stamping a plank floor with the mark of a peg.

Salvaged or reclaimed wood floors are gaining in popularity among log-home builders and owners. This interest is partly due to a sense of responsibility to recycle in order to conserve natural resources and an appreciation for the beauty of antique materials. Reclaimed wood that has been rescued from nineteenth-century factories, rural structures, such as trestle bridges and barns, is replaned and graded before it is used again.

Although building with recycled materials can be costly, many log-home owners like the idea that there is a history behind them. Also, the beauty of reclaimed wood lies in the imperfections that come with

time—the weathered finish, the worm holes, and nail marks. Artisans and home-owners who choose to work with salvaged materials do so because the aged patina of old wood cannot be thoroughly duplicated in anything that is new.

Laminate

When your purist side says "wood" but your practical side knows that you need a less-expensive alternative, a look-alike laminate floor might be just the thing. Although laminate flooring may not be the first choice for a log home, it is an option especially in the kitchen or bathroom because it's easy to clean with a mop or broom and it resists stains.

Laminate flooring is made from paper impregnated with melamine, an organic resin that is bonded to a core of particle-board, fiberboard, or other wood by-products. Laminate can provide the look you desire along with practicality.

Carpeting & Rugs

The warmth of carpeting underfoot is a plus in a log home, especially in northern or mountain locations. Because of its luxurious look and wearing abilities, wall-to-wall carpeting is primarily used in log-home bedrooms and other private areas. Carpeting is available in a wide range of colors and textures. Give some thought to the other furnishings in the room when you're selecting carpeting. Will the carpet be a backdrop or the primary color component in the room?

Commercial carpeting, once reserved for contract installations, has become popular for residential use. The low tight weave is designed for easy maintenance, yet it is warm and comfortable. This type of carpeting would work well in a loft area or a finished attic or basement.

Cheap carpeting doesn't wear well and will have to be replaced after a short time. Buy the best you can afford and remember that a large part of the cost is installation.

Area rugs are a great way to add color, pattern, and texture to a room and you can changed them with the seasons. When choosing one, think about the size of the room. A rug with a border will make a room seem smaller. Using too many small rugs in a room will create a spotty look.

Rugs can also be used to define furniture groupings or conversation areas in a room. Patterned area rugs will enliven a scheme, but cautiously choose prints that are based on your overall color palette. Otherwise the rug could overwhelm the room. Painted floor cloths, once used by early settlers as an inexpensive substitute for rugs, are made of canvas that is painted and coated with linseed oil or polyurethane. Buy one at a crafts fair or paint your own. They are especially popular for country-style kitchens because of their handcrafted look, water resistance, and wearability.

Ceramic Tile

Ceramic tile has become a popular flooring choice throughout the house. Kiln-fired and made from clay, quarry tile is usually unglazed. Terra-cotta is the most desirable of this type. Quarry tile can be oiled or waxed to bring out its warm luster. Available in earthy tones of brick red, the wide variety of colors and textures allows tile to work in virtually any room. In warmer climates, especially in the Southeast and Southwest where the temperature can soar most of the year, the cool touch of a ceramic-tile floor can offer welcome relief from the heat. Just be sure to choose tile that is specifically designed to be used on the floor.

ABOVE: Area rugs are a great way to define furniture groupings in a room. The best part is their flexibility—rugs can be moved from room to room and changed with the seasons.

BELOW: Wood, slate, and concrete are popular flooring materials for log homes. Unfortunately, they can also be tiring. Adding an area rug with padding is one way to alleviate this problem.

TOP: Instead of an area rug, this room features a river-stone inset. The rough texture of the stone provides a nice contrast to the sleek contemporary setting.

ABOVE: Available in earthy tones of red, brown, and gray, tiles can provide color and texture to log interiors. This entranceway features an inlaid tile "bear rug" on the floor.

Concrete

At one time considered acceptable flooring only for the garage or basement, concrete is now a popular choice for residential use all through the house. As a flooring material, it is extremely durable and inexpensive when compared to other masonry flooring such as ceramic tile and stone. It has a modern, industrial look that is perfect with a contemporary-style log home or one that is particularly rustic.

"Concrete is great for lower-level floors and especially for use with radiant heat," says Bob Marcom. "Because of its weight, I would avoid installing concrete flooring on upper levels."

Like wood, concrete is versatile and available in a wide variety of finishes and textures, including smooth; acid stained, which creates a mottled effect; or rough stucco. When wet, concrete can be imprinted with designs or scored to look like tile. Designs can also be added to poured concrete by inserting wood strips or tile in geometric patterns.

You can also color concrete with paint or stain. An acrylic-urethane polymer stain is available in a full palette of colors. After the floor dries, seal it with several coats of a nonyellowing polyurethane. If you like an antique look, use wax, which will turn slightly golden over time.

Stone

Slate, flagstone, brick, and limestone are perfectly suited to the earthy ambiance of a log home. In its natural state, stone is water resistant and very durable. When properly sealed against stains, stone flooring requires little maintenance. However, it is hard, cold, and noisy, and once set, difficult to remove.

Regardless of the design, keep the overall look subtle. If the floor pattern is strong, the rest of the room must compensate so that the floor does not dominate. Remember: a well-designed room is balanced so that all of the elements are in harmony with each other.

Windows

The original pioneer cabin had a few tiny windows designed to keep out the hot sun and the winter cold. Today's light-filled home has many windows. After logs, windows can be the second-largest building expense. The latest designs in double- and triple-glazed windows have changed the rules of log-home design, allowing builders to open up the interiors to natural light, ventilation, and views.

"When choosing window frames for our homes, we suggest a metal-clad exterior frame with a wood interior frame," says Mike Nelson, Owner, Nelson Design Group, Jonesboro, Arkansas. "Metal cladding protects against the elements and the interior wood frame maintains the integrity of the logs."

Windows have become an architectural asset as well, playing a major part in shaping a home's personality. "When installing windows in a log home, we try to use a similar size and shape on the same side of the house." Says Nelson. "Unless there are utili-

SMART IDEA

The natural color of eco-friendly cork makes it an attractive alternative for wood flooring in a log home. Cork is not slippery and is a great insulator against heat and cold. In addition to being one of the most comfortable and resilient flooring surfaces, it absorbs sound effectively.

Tieback curtain panels with swag valances provide a slightly formal, traditional touch to this log-home living room. The treatment is designed to frame the window without obstructing the breathtaking view.

tarian reasons, we mix two styles. For instance, in one case we might use casement windows for the bedrooms and an awning-type window for the sunroom with fixed glass at the top and an operable unit on the bottom. But for the most part, uniformity is the preferred way to go."

Now that many log-home owners expect to pay a high premium for views, windows have become a top priority.

Window Siting

Perhaps as important as the view, another consideration is the direction of natural light. Where will the sun rise and set in

each room? Strong sunlight can cause serious ultraviolet (UV) damage to both fabric and wood, including the log walls, fading them over time.

Depending on where you live, the amount of sunlight that comes indoors can also affect your heating and air-conditioning bill. Keep in mind that east-facing rooms will get morning light, south-facing rooms will bathe in the midday sun, and west-facing windows get strong late afternoon sunlight. Northern windows get very little if any direct light.

Fortunately, the window-manufacturing industry has developed several types of energy-saving designs that allow you to forgo any covering and maximize your natural light. Tinted glass, multiple layers of glazing, low-E coatings, or windows with gas-filled spaces between the panes are just a few of the options offered to homeowners today.

Window Dressing

If privacy or energy factors are important, you can use window treatments to help. When choosing curtains, make note of how far you will be able to retract the panels, especially where there is minimal wall space around a window or when you want to maximize a view.

Shades offer a variety of options for dressing a window. Some will provide privacy while blocking light, others, such as sunscreen shades, are made of a washable, flat, synthetic material that is extremely durable. When lowered you can still see through them, but they will keep your room cool and safe from harmful UV rays. Many window shades and screens can be motorized—an especially helpful option if you have floor-to-ceiling windows. If you prefer to control the sun from the outside of your house, installing retractable awnings is a smart option.

OPPOSITE: Unobtrusive shades are versatile. They provide light control when the home-owners need it, or they can be raised, as they are here, to let in the sun and view.

RIGHT: Bleached-log walls look contemporary in this off-white living room. Neutral palettes such as this one can be easily changed with the addition of colorful accessories.

Looking Up, Not Out

If a standard window isn't practical or the room is lacking a view, consider *skylights* or *roof windows*. They are a great source of light and air and when properly installed will keep out the elements. Height and operability are no longer a problem because roof windows are available with remote controls that can be programmed to open and close both the window and the window covering.

Be sure to discuss all of your window options, including decorative treatments, with your architect or designer at the very beginning of the building process, not after the walls have been constructed.

The Power of Color

When it comes to color, log interiors provide a perfect background for a bevy of rich, nature-inspired schemes. Just as the type, size, and color of logs define the style of the room, so will they set the tone for the room's overall color palette.

Light can be the most important element in creating a successful color scheme. You can be guided by studying the room and the type and amount of natural light. Is it reflecting the warm sun from the south or a cool bluish light from the north?

Warm hues are the color of sunshine—yellows, reds, and oranges. *Cool hues* are found in the grass, sea, and sky—blues, greens, and violets. If a room has a southern exposure with warm-tone log walls,

create balance between these natural attributes by using a combination of cool and neutral colors. Use a warm color scheme in a part of the house that faces north in order to compensate for the lack of natural light and the cool atmosphere.

It also helps to keep in mind the change of seasons. The intensity of light will look different depending on the time of year. Because the days are shorter during the winter months, more supplemental light is required indoors. Choose a color scheme that works well in both natural and artificial light. You can also change the colors in a room to coincide with and complement the seasons by using different throw rugs, blankets, and slipcovers to keep the look fresh with the passing months.

Color as a Mood Changer

One of the most important goals of decorating a log home is to create a comfortable, relaxed, and cheerful environment. Before you dec-

orate, think about how you want to feel in the room. Color can affect your mood, create energy, or bring a sense of calm. Combinations of light colors can make a small area feel spacious, while darker tones can make a large space cozier and intimate.

Just as important as the room's location and light, is its function. Will the room be a place for friends and family to gather, or a quiet retreat for relaxation? Warm colors are conducive to energy and activities, a good choice for kitchens and family rooms. Cool colors are more relaxing and soothing, the type of mood you might choose for a bedroom, bath, or den.

COLOR QUESTIONNAIRE

- How will the room be used?
- What kind of mood do you want to convey?
- How much natural light is there?
- What time of day will you use the room?
- Are there any flat surfaces—walls, doors, or built-ins—where you can add color?
- Are there architectural features—moldings, a fireplace—to consider?

Go Natural

Throughout a log home, natural materials and organic colors are important because of the strong connection between the interior spaces and the outdoors. The best color palettes are inspired by nature. These color combinations already exist in perfect harmony in the woodland foliage, berries, and grasses of the changing seasons, for example. Or look at a waterscape for inspiration—a lakeside color combination of blue water and sky against the lush greens and yellows of a summer forest. The rainbow of hues found in a field of wildflowers can also provide you with ideas for combining colors.

Don't forget that the greens, browns, golds, and terra-cottas that are the traditional earth colors are also easy to live with in a log home. Comfortable and relaxing, these hues work particularly well in living and dining rooms and studies where their warm tones create a familiar and inviting environment.

SMART IDEA

Try to have only one dominant color in the room. Bringing two colors of equal importance into a room will only confuse the eye. Never use a color once; always repeat a color throughout the room. This will create rhythm and harmony in a color scheme.

OPPOSITE: This Western-style great room comes alive with a mix of bright yellow walls, white logs, and natural wood.

ABOVE: When it comes to log-home living, sometimes the best color palettes are taken from the rich browns of the wood.

Ready-Made Color Schemes

Another favorite way to devise a color scheme is to incorporate the hues of a favorite print fabric, rug, or work of art. This is practically a fail-proof method because a professional designer or artist has already worked out the color harmonies.

Working with colors in the design you've chosen, find matching paint chips and lay them out on a white board. Looking at your design, start with the dominant color in the pattern and use it for the largest areas of your room.

The next strongest colors in the pattern should be for the smaller pieces of furniture and the window treatments. Limit the brightest or most intense colors for the accents—colors you will pick up for accessories and works of art.

Next, put together a sample board with these colors as your guide. Add and remove things as you try different looks, colors, and textures. Once you've made your final selections, use rubber cement to attach all of the paint chips, swatches of fabrics, carpets, or rugs, and photos of furniture or surface materials to the board. Then view it in the appropriate room at different times of the day under natural and artificial lighting conditions.

As a guide, keep in mind that the best colors, textures, and materials to use in a log home are the natural and classic ones, not those that are dictated by fashion trends. If you do, the result will be casual and comfortable without sacrificing timeless elegance.

ACCENT WITH COLOR

- Hang a quilt on the wall.
- Drape a Navajo rug over the back of a sofa.
- Display a colorful dish collection.
- Use bright accent tiles on the floor and walls.
- Install a stained-glass window.
- Add colorful cornices, curtains, or shades on the windows.
- Color the white chinking in the walls with a wood stain.

Kitchens with Heart

3

O f all the rooms in a log house, the kitchen presents a unique decorating challenge because it is usually open to the dining and living rooms. An open design, which on the one hand creates a feeling of spaciousness, also allows for a full and unobstructed view of the kitchen area during the preparation of food and any messiness that may generate. One solution is to add an island or peninsula, which can camouflage the work area without closing up the layout.

Birch-bark cabinets and polished-oak countertops tie into this cabin's rustic look. A raised breakfast bar at one end separates the kitchen's work area from the adjacent living space.

Traditionally, the kitchen in a pioneer's log cabin was part of a larger communal "great" room that was used for eating, socializing, and maybe for sleeping, too. This tradition is one of the reasons you will rarely, if ever, find a closed-off kitchen in a new log home regardless of its size. Despite the desirability of open space, there is a still a need to create visual separation between the kitchen and the rest of the great room. Most designers will define the kitchen area by subtle hints of detachment, such as a dropped ceiling painted a different color than the living area. Installing a contrasting flooring material will also create a visual partition.

Space-defining furnishings, such as low cabinets, peninsulas, or islands, are other popular separating devices. Log posts placed at the entrance of the kitchen can serve as dividers, without closing off an area. On the other hand, using colors and patterns in the kitchen that blend with the rest of the great room will maintain design continuity.

Determine Your Needs

Spontaneity can be fun, but not when it comes to designing your kitchen. Planning ahead will save you from expensive mistakes later. "Design your log-home kitchen before you begin any construction," says Nancy Frasier, of Frasier's Kitchen Showplace, in Rhinelander, Wisconsin. "We ask clients first to put together a collection of photos of their ideal kitchen. This process helps identify what is most important to their lifestyle."

Define Your Lifestyle

Start by considering your daily activities and how you want the room to function. Is anyone in your household a gourmet cook? Do you like to entertain? If so, who prepares the meals—you or a caterer? Or are you more inclined to have friends over for potluck dinners? Do you like to bake? The answers to these questions will be important factors in your kitchen's design. If you like to cook, professional-style appliances

ABOVE: Light-wood cabinetry was designed to seamlessly integrate with the log walls. Stainless-steel appliances and granite countertops give the room a contemporary flavor.

OPPOSITE: A large island separates this kitchen from the adjoining great room, adds storage space, and provides an additional work surface with a cooktop.

might be on your list of must-haves. If you entertain frequently, consider installing two sinks for prepping and clean up. Also think about adding an extra dishwasher or a pair of dishwasher drawers. A baker will want to include a bake center with a minimum of 36 to 42 inches of counter and cabinet space and specially designed storage for pans and utensils. This counter space may also include a marble slab for rolling out pastry. Kitchen designers recommend making this counter 4 to 6 inches lower than the height of your elbow when it's bent at a 90-degree angle.

In other words, list what you will need in your new kitchen, then sit down with a designer who will help make it all fit.

Get The Right Help

Kitchens require a specially trained professional. In this case, it's a Certified Kitchen Designer (CKD), someone who not only has an eye for decorating but also has the training and experience to deal with the numerous design issues, such as arranging space and choosing cabinetry, materials, and appliances, that come up in the course of planning a kitchen.

All of these considerations make the kitchen one of the most complicated rooms to plan in any house, but in a log home, it comes with an extra set of hurdles. Remember that you are dealing with solid-log walls in many cases, so any electrical wiring, lighting, plumbing, and appliance placement is going to have to be carefully planned ahead of time. Even cabinets will have to be meticulously scored into the walls and expertly fitted around log beams in the ceiling.

OPPOSITE TOP: Knotty-pine walls, floors, and cabinets give this kitchen a bright, fresh look. In this spacious layout, an island shortens the distance between work areas.

OPPOSITE BOTTOM: Bleached-wood cabinets and stainless-steel appliances put a fresh face on this Adirondack-themed room. Working closely with the homeowners, the designer created a custom kitchen complete with a TV that can be viewed from the island's breakfast bar.

BELOW: Red cabinets provide a pleasing contrast to the log walls while creating a visual separation between the kitchen and living room.

Configuring Work Space

Creating an efficient workstation is an integral part of kitchen planning. Start with the work triangle, an imaginary path that connects the kitchen's three primary task areas—the sink, refrigerator, and cooktop. "The traditional triangle has morphed over the years with the addition of dishwasher drawers and compact refrigerator systems," says Nancy Frasier. "Thanks to this new technology the modern kitchen layouts are much more flexible."

Two of the most popular layouts for the log home are the L shape and the U shape.

The L-shape. This plan places the kitchen on two perpendicular walls. The L-shape usually consists of one long and one short "leg" and lends itself to an efficient work triangle. It's also flexible enough for two cooks to work simultaneously without getting in each other's way. Another advantage to this layout is the opportunity for incorporating an island into the floor plan, if space allows.

The U-shape. Cabinets, counters, and appliances are all arranged along three walls in a U configuration. The greatest benefit of this plan is the openness and easy traffic flow it allows. Some experts believe that a U-shape kitchen is the most efficient design, but others will argue it's a matter of personal preference.

Save or Splurge

Whether you have unlimited resources or are working with a tight budget, it's smart to establish a sound financial plan for your kitchen project. Careful budgeting will help you stay on course so that you don't spend too much on this one part of the house. Because of the wide variety of cabinets, faucets, appliances, fixtures, and materials, the kitchen—more than any other room— is where you will have more choices to make than you ever imagined.

LEFT: Steel and glass pendant lamps, inspired by old factory fixtures, provide a warm glow over this kitchen's cleanup zone, which features two sinks and a dark-slate countertop.

OPPOSITE: Plain-panel wood cabinets with sleek chrome hardware, stainless-steel appliances, granite countertops, and high-tech strip lights give this log kitchen its modern aesthetic.

Surfaces

The walls, floors, cabinet fronts, and countertops can help to define your style. Your personal choices should be based on what you like and what you need. Introducing color to these surfaces can enliven your log-home kitchen by creating relief from the natural shades and textures of the wood. Color can actually enhance its beauty by providing a much-needed contrast to the dominant beige or brown scheme. Where can you add color if it's not on the walls? Look at other surfaces in the room—the cabinets, countertop, and the floor.

If you're not sure about using color on the cabinets, you could reserve it for just a detail or use it on one section in a run of cabinets. Feeling more daring? Introduce color on your countertop or flooring. Neither of these is necessarily easy or inexpensive to replace, so avoid trendy colors that will date your kitchen.

As a rule of thumb, use no more than three colors in the room. For interest, apply them in varying shades and tints. If you are set on using a single color, liven it up by adding pattern and texture.

Countertops

Selecting a countertop material is not as simple as it once was because now there are infinitely more choices in color, pattern, and texture thanks to new materials and applications. The trend is to use more than one material, specifying a type based on the function at hand. For example, you could use a solid-surfacing material in one area of

LIGHTING

Kitchen designers recommend that a lighting plan include both task and ambient illumination. Task lighting will brighten specific activities, such as reading a recipe or rolling out dough in a baking center, while ambient light is for general or overall illumination. Track lighting or spotlights that let you aim light in a specific, narrow direction are good bets for task lighting. Under-cabinet lighting is a good example. Ambient lighting is usually provided by an overhead fixture or a series of recessed canisters that provide an overall level of soft, diffused light. Besides incandescent bulbs, including halogen, you can choose more energy-efficient and longer-lasting full-spectrum fluorescent bulbs that simulate daylight. They can improve color rendition and lessen eye fatigue.

the kitchen, a marble insert at the bake center, and granite next to the cooktop. Or you could choose one countertop material for cabinets along the wall and another for the island counter.

In addition to enhancing the function of your work surface, the countertop material you choose can underpin your log-home's decorating theme. (For a rundown on countertop materials, see "Countertop Options," on the opposite page.)

Because of their natural appearance, tile and stone products, such as soapstone, granite, and slate, have become popular choices for the log home kitchen. If you decide on stone, consider using a honed or matte finish for a more rustic look.

CLASSIC TRIANGLE

Almost everyone has heard of the classic kitchen work triangle. Basically it is a plan that puts three major zones—cooking, refrigeration, and cleanup—at three different points of a triangle. The spatial relationship between these zones and how they relate to other areas in the kitchen are what make the room an efficient workspace. In the classic work triangle, the distance between any pair of the three centers is no longer than 9 feet and no less than 4 feet.

Natural stone can be used to face just about any vertical surface, such as this rustic kitchen island featuring a handcrafted wood countertop.

COUNTERTOP OPTIONS

You have numerous countertop choices today. After you've read about the attributes of each one, you can decide which ones may be right for you.

• **Plastic Laminate** Inexpensive, relatively easy to install, and available in a vast array of colors and patterns, plastic laminate can mimic more expensive surface choices. It resists stains, water, and mild abrasion, but can be chipped or scratched by sharp knives.

• **Solid Surfacing** Solid surfacing is a synthetic material that is initially expensive, costing almost as much as granite or marble, but wears long and well. The material is completely impervious to water, and you can repair any dents or abrasions with a light sanding. It comes in colors or faux-stone finishes. The solid-color core means it can be carved, inlaid, shaped, and molded.

• **Composite Material** Produced by binding stone chips (typically quartz) to powders and resins, composite is extremely hard. Its textured and variegated look has a remarkable resemblance to stone except the patterns formed are more constant and the choice of colors is greater. Composite stone is heat- and scratch-resistant and easy to clean. Price-wise, it's almost comparable to stone.

• **Ceramic Tile** A perennial favorite, ceramic tile is durable and offers the greatest opportunity for adding color, pattern, and texture to a log-home kitchen.

• **Granite** One of the most popular stone countertops used in today's kitchen, granite is a hard stone and practically nonporous. This igneous rock has a visual crystalline, coarse-grain texture with a speckled effect formed from quartz, feldspar, and mica. It is available in a variety of natural colors as well as almost pure black and almost pure white.

• **Slate** A richly textured, durable stone for counters, slate costs less than granite yet performs as well or better. Available in solid earthy tones of greens, black, grays, and purples, the surface often features bits of mica and other mineral deposits.

• **Soapstone and Limestone** Unlike the refined look of granite, these materials have a rustic, textured appeal that works well in a log-home kitchen. As with all natural materials, soapstone and limestone are absorbent and must be sealed periodically.

• **Wood** A favorite for log-home kitchens, natural wood can be stained a variety of colors. Wood has a tendency to expand, contract, and warp if exposed to water, however. To protect a wood countertop, you will have to seal it with a finish of varnish or lacquer, and then refinish it periodically.

• **Concrete** Durable and heat resistant, concrete can be easily custom fitted into the shape of your kitchen's counter configuration. Depending on how you finish it, a concrete countertop can look sleek and modern or rustic. Color can be added to concrete, and some applications are carved, routed, or inlaid with tile or stone.

• **Paper** This sustainable composite material is made from recycled paper and other fibers that have been impregnated with a nonpetroleum-based resin to create a heat-resistant surface that is very durable. Paper-based countertops come in a variety of earthy colors.

Flooring

As with every other product you select for the kitchen, flooring plays a role in establishing style, especially in the log cabin. You can use flooring to visually separate the kitchen from the rest of the living area. This can be done with material, color, or both. The choice of kitchen flooring usually comes down to purism versus practicality.

Log-cabin homeowners are usually drawn to natural materials, of which there are several options. Popular choices are *wood, cork, stone,* or *tile.* Generally, a material that is hard, such as stone or ceramic tile, can be uncomfortable to stand on for long periods of time. Cork and wood are more comfortable because they are flexible. Therefore consider your cooking style when you select a flooring material for the kitchen. Maintenance should also affect your decision. If your kitchen is a busy place with kids, pets, and friends, turning it into a heavy traffic area, forget purism and consider the practical side of laminate or vinyl flooring.

Sinks and Faucets

What could be more basic to a kitchen than a sink and faucet? Yet in today's modern world, there's practically nothing basic about them. Style comes in all price ranges, but high-performance technology is accompanied by an equally high price tag.

Sinks

These receptacles come in all sizes, shapes, and colors, and they are typically fabricated from enameled cast iron, metal, composite material, solid-surfacing material, concrete, or stone. The shape and color of the sink will depend on the style of the room. The trend is to include the largest sink that you can accommodate within the confines of your space. A favorite in log homes is the deep farm-style (or exposed apron) sink

that is available in a range of patterns and colors. Two- and three-bowl configurations that let you separate dishes and glassware are also gaining in popularity.

There are five types of sink-installation styles to consider.

Undermounted. If you want a smooth look, an undermounted sink may be for you. The bowl is attached underneath the countertop.

Integral. As the word implies, an integral sink is fabricated from the same material as the countertop—stone, concrete, or solid-surfacing material.

Self-rimming or flush-mounted. A self-rimmed sink has a rolled edge that is mounted on the countertop.

Rimmed. Unlike a self-rimming sink, this type requires a flat metal strip to seal the sink to the countertop.

Tile-in. Used with a tiled countertop, the sink's rim is flush with the tiled surface. Grout seals the sink to the surrounding countertop area.

OPPOSITE: Polished-stone counters can be costly, but elegant. If stone is not in your price range, an affordable alternative is ceramic tile.

ABOVE: This handsome single-lever faucet with a pullout sprayer is perfectly matched to the black drop-in double-bowl sink.

BELOW: Inserting a red painted cabinet with an exposed-apron sink into the counter adds both color and interest to this country-style kitchen.

Faucets

No longer just a conduit for water, today's faucet selections offer beauty as well as function to a kitchen. An excellent example is the *pot-filler faucet*, which is mounted to the wall over the cooktop. Some versions have a pullout spout; others come with a double- or triple-jointed arm that can be bent to reach up and down, or swiveled, allowing the cook to pull the faucet over to a pot on the farthest burner.

State-of-the-art technology in faucets gives you not only much more control over water use but better performance and more extensive finishes as well. Some specialty features to look for include pullout faucet heads, retractable sprayers, hot- and cold-water dispensing, single-lever control, and built-in water purifier to enhance taste.

When you design your sink and faucet area, don't be sidetracked by good looks alone. Instead, compare the size of your biggest pots to see whether the sink you're considering will accommodate them. If it won't and you can't install something deeper, pair the sink with a pullout goose-neck faucet.

ABOVE: A combination of light-wood cabinets, a slate-tile backsplash, black granite countertops, and a stainless-steel sink gives this kitchen its rustic charm. A pot rack in the shape of a fish adds a whimsical touch to the room.

LEFT: A terra-cotta-hue farmhouse sink and single-handle faucet in a rubbed-bronze finish combine with stone countertops and light-wood cabinets for a quaint, yet traditional, American-country aesthetic.

OPPOSITE: Storage is a key element in this kitchen that features dishwasher drawers and a country-style built-in hutch. A soapstone sink, granite countertop, and cabinets with bead-board detailing underscore the refined look.

Planning Your Storage

It's not a matter of creating more space in your new kitchen, but making better use of the existing space. This will require careful analysis of every area of the kitchen for its storage needs. Point-of-use storage saves both steps and time and is a common denominator in a well-planned kitchen. It makes sense to keep cookware near the range, dishes and glasses close to the sink, and dish-washing and food items between these workstations. To keep clutter at a minimum, include space for utility rooms—pantry, broom closet, and laundry room.

Cabinetry

Cabinets not only have the greatest impact on a kitchen's appearance, good cabinetry outfitted with an assortment of organizing options can also make it a more efficient and neater place. But keep in mind that because log-home cabinetry has to be custom made to the designer's specifications, it will also consume about 40 percent of your kitchen budget. So before making any expensive decisions or costly mistakes, investigate all of the various cabinetry options that are available to you.

The overall look in your kitchen will be largely influenced by the style of cabinetry you select. Finding a style that suits you is like shopping for furniture. In fact, like furnishings, many cabinet designs can convey

HARDWARE

Another way to emphasize your kitchen's decorative style is with hardware. From handsome reproductions in brass, pewter, wrought iron, or bronze, a variety of shapes and designs are available to dress up your cabinets and doors.

Designed to stretch this kitchen's limited space, the island does double duty by providing a centrally located spot for prep tasks and extra storage.

a rustic or country look with crown molding, plate racks, and paneled doors in vintage finishes reminiscent of furnishings found in early log cabins.

Cabinets with color accents in one or two hues can look great when paired with natural wood tones. Growing in popularity in the log-home kitchen is the use of translucent color glazes and distressed finishing techniques, such as wire brushing and rubbed-through color. They add another dimension to the appeal of hand-craftsmanship. Homeowners who love the look of classic wood cabinets can stain them a darker or lighter color to stand out against the log walls.

Islands

The kitchen island is a modern version of the original pioneer farm table, a place where food was prepared and eaten. Today's island can serve several functions: separating the work areas from adjacent living spaces, housing a sink, dishwasher, and small appliances, and providing space for snacks and cookbook storage. The style of the island is usually related to the cabinets, but it doesn't have to be. An island is a good place to add a touch of color, highlighting it as a focal point in the room. And keep in mind that an island doesn't have to be permanent; it can also be a simple freestanding farm table with open storage below it.

FREESTANDING FURNITURE

Although cabinets and islands will take up a lot of the floor space, consider including freestanding individual pieces of furniture as well. Cupboards, chests of drawers, and antique hutches can increase your storage space and add a warm, timeless look to the room.

Appliances

When it comes to choosing appliances, there has never been more variety in every price category. With so many options, it's especially important to analyze your needs before shopping. Take into consideration your family size, how often company visits, the types of food you typically prepare, and how much cooking you do.

Next to cabinets, appliances will take up a large chunk of your overall budget. Because most appliances will last 15 to 20 years, it is important to choose the model and size that is right for your lifestyle now—and for the not too distant future.

Because the kitchen is open to the living area, log-home owners usually tend to shy away from massive refrigerators or dishwashers that strongly announce their presence in a room. Fortunately these items can be very attractively hidden behind custom panels that match the cabinetry or made to disappear behind refrigerator and dishwasher drawers that can be placed anywhere in the room. Except for a stainless-steel professional-style range or cooktop (that can offer a welcome visual relief from too much wood), many appliances can now literally blend into the woodwork.

BELOW: A pair of built-in ovens, a large refrigerator and freezer, and a professional-style range is something that serious cooks will appreciate. Here, the stainless-steel appliances provide visual respite from the wood walls, floor, cabinets, and ceiling.

OPPOSITE: This log-home kitchen boasts a large cooking hearth with a pair of electric ovens and a gas cooktop. Pieces of the granite countertop were used to create the inlay design on the ceramic-tile backsplash. Lighting and the exhaust system are hidden by the log arch.

A mix of sleek materials and bleached-log walls create a modern-day Western look.

There are two basic questions you'll have to answer up front about your cooking equipment. What kind of fuel will you use (gas or electric) and will it be a configuration of separate cooktop and oven units or a large all-in-one range? You can also combine fuels in the same appliance (called "dual fuel").

If you are interested in adding a period look to your log-home kitchen, check out vintage appliances. There are several appliance-restoration companies around the country that can supply you with a refurbished and fully functioning refrigerator or

DISPLAYING COLLECTIBLES

When it comes to collections, the rule is to keep it simple and avoid cutesy clutter. A touch of whimsy is fine and always looks at home in a log kitchen, especially when it is handcrafted. Don't feel obligated to display only kitchen-related items.

stove. These early appliances, usually dating from 1910 to the 1960s, can be expensive. But if you are into investing in antiques this might be something to investigate.

On the other hand, if you want the look of a late-nineteenth or early twentieth-century appliance that functions at a twenty-first century level, think about a reproduction of a vintage appliance. It's a way to get that nostalgic look without the expensive price tag. You can also get all of the modern conveniences and efficiency in a retro-style appliance including a choice of contemporary colors.

NEAT IDEAS TO CONSIDER

• If you have kids or lots of company, install a compact refrigerator for cold drinks under a counter. This beverage center will save a lot of daily wear and tear on your main refrigerator.

• Plan to have a walk-in pantry. With all of the big box stores today, you can save money in the long run by buying bulk. In addition, you won't have to worry about being snowed in for the week if you are prepared with extra staples and food.

• Do you drink lots of tea and coffee? If so, investing in a built-in espresso/hot water machine might be the practical way to go.

• Stretch your cooking space by installing an island consisting of a prep sink, wine cooler, convection/microwave oven, dishwasher drawers, compact refrigerator, and a pullout chopping block.

• Keep meals hot with a built-in warming drawer designed to maintain foods at the right temperature until you're ready to serve them. This appliance is especially handy during large dinner parties.

4

Bath and Bedroom

oday's bathroom has gone beyond its original utilitarian nature and has become more of a haven, a place to relax and refresh. This is especially true in the log home. Filled with a warm uncomplicated atmosphere that is in tune with nature, the serenity that fills the log home continues into this retreat. Here is the place where, surrounded by candles, fragrant soaps, and fluffy towels, one can soak away the rigors of the day.

OPPOSITE: Simplicity in design combined with skilled craftsmanship is apparent in this Arts and Craft-style guest bath featuring hand-hewn dovetail-style logs and informal furnishings.

ABOVE: Topped with marble, this custom vanity was designed with a large window positioned over the grooming area to provide a view of the magnificent mountain range.

How many bathrooms should you have? As with other important design questions, the answer will depend on the size of your family, your lifestyle, and the size of your home. Fortunately you can solve this dilemma before investing in a single fixture. By carefully working out the designs on paper, you can plan as many bathrooms as you need. Shared bathrooms should cater to the style and color preferences of everyone in the household.

Family Needs

There are certain elements that a full bath must include: a toilet, tub, shower, lavatory, and storage. Once you have made your basic selections, start thinking about a look or theme. To maintain a harmonious visual flow, choose the same colors for all of the permanent fixtures.

As a rule of thumb, designers suggest planning at least one bathroom for the main floor of the house. If that will be the master bath, consider installing a half-bath or powder room—a toilet and a lav—for guests. If space and your budget allows, plan for one bathroom or at least a half-bath for every guest room. In addition to the master bath, there should be at least another full bath for family and guests. This will ensure privacy for everyone.

Powder Rooms. Guest bath, half-bath, it has multiple names—and it may be the most efficient room in the house—providing just what you need often in tight quarters. You can also find small-scaled fixtures specifically designed for the limited-size of most powder rooms—3 x 5 feet is not uncommon, but size ultimately depends on the home's layout and the available space.

A carefully devised floor plan makes a difference in a compact room. To save on usable floor space the doors can swing out instead of into a small bathroom. Another space-saving idea is a pocket door.

Because the powder room is often for guests and located on the ground floor, ensure privacy by locating it away from the living areas.

A mixture of earthiness and elegance, this large master bath suite has a cozy sitting area, candelabras, a custom-designed vanity with storage, and an old-fashioned soaking tub.

The Family Bath. You need to aim more for efficiency as well as comfort in a bathroom that will be shared by several people. The family bath may not be the place to relax for long periods of time because it's usually a room where shorter occupancy is appreciated. This is not to say that the family bath cannot be a comfortable haven for as long as it is being used. It's still a place where you can shut the door and be alone. Include refreshing colors, rich surfaces, and handsome state-of-the-art fixtures.

If there are space restrictions and the bath seems cramped, bring in lots of natural light, good artificial lighting, and use translucent partitions made of glass blocks or etched glass. Anything that divides separate areas of the bath while allowing light to enter will help ease that closed-in feeling.

Master Bath. The whole idea of a master bath is to create that sought-after getaway—the home version of a European spa. When designing the floor plan of your log-home dream bath, consider the clearance that is required to accommodate and comfortably use the fixtures. Here's a place to truly pamper yourself. Some popular amenities include a hydromassage tub, separate shower with steam and multiple massage showerheads, and dual sinks on opposite sides of the room. Some of the best layouts include adjacent dressing rooms or walk-in closets. Couples want to share a master bedroom and bath, but they may also want privacy while getting dressed without tripping over their mates.

With the future in mind, incorporate some features of universal design into a bathroom. Install grab bars and use lever-style hardware instead of knobs on doors and faucets. Make doorways a minimum of 32 inches wide, and leave enough space, a 5-foot diameter, in the center of the room for a wheelchair to make a complete turn.

Your Personal View

If your home has several beautiful vistas, plan to have at least one window installed in the master bath, preferably over the tub. Make this view of the outdoors part of your relaxing back-to-nature experience. Unwind in the tub while soaking in the view—what could be better? If privacy is a concern,

Designing Ideas

When considering style, take a cue from the rest of your home. The one transitional element will be the log walls, which will create a visual bridge from room to room. The bathroom in a log home is more likely to be characterized by a selective nostalgia—taking attractive elements of the past and updating them with modern technology. For example, outfitting an old-fashioned freestanding claw-foot bathtub with a modern hand-held shower.

Decorate the bathroom as you would any room in the house. If your style is Adirondack, accessorize the room with twig furnishings, cabin-themed rugs with bears, elk, or pine-cone motifs, and color-coordinated towels.

For an American-country look, consider gingham-check curtains and baskets for storing hand towels. Decorate with a country-themed wallpaper or a stencil if there is drywall in the bathroom.

For a Southwestern look, add some clever props, such as a wood ladder instead of a towel rack. You could also incorporate tile surfaces in Southwestern colors of turquoise, coral, terra-cotta, and sand, or cover a section of drywall in stucco. Accent the look with earthy pottery.

The bathroom can be a place where you can retreat comfortably and spend quiet time alone. Quiet colors will enhance that quality. Also, incorporate living plants into the room. Tropical plants, such as orchids and bromeliads will add color and thrive on the humidity. Palm plants and ferns are good choices, too.

Decoratively speaking, you don't have to take things too seriously. This can be the room in the house that breaks with conformity. Make it the place to savor privacy and quiet moments alone. Try experimenting with colors, displaying artwork, and quirky collectibles.

SMART IDEA

When choosing accessories and artwork, use caution when displaying originals. Dampness from steam and water may result in a fatal case of mildew, especially if there is not enough ventilation. Check out some of the many water-resistant or bath-friendly accessories on the market, many of which would suit a log-cabin ambiance. Or hang reproductions that are inexpensive and can be easily replaced if damaged.

ABOVE: White plaster walls, a lithograph printed on rustic boards, and an arched doorway give this log-home master bathroom a Southwestern look.

OPPOSITE: A William Morris-inspired wallpaper mixed with a traditional-style canopied vanity adds a dressy look to this design.

consider covering the window with a double-cord control shade that allows you to adjust the shade in two directions—either from the bottom up or from the top down. This feature is handy if you want to lower the top of the shade to gaze at the sky while maintaining privacy.

OPPOSITE TOP: A mix of rustic and romantic, this bath features a tiled wall that extends into a walk-in shower. Accent pieces, such as the antler chandelier and the antique chest, add warmth to the room.

OPPOSITE BOTTOM LEFT: The perfect getaway, tucked away into an alcove and surrounded by warm wood walls, this cozy bath features an old-fashioned claw-foot tub. There's a separate shower to the left of the tub.

OPPOSITE BOTTOM RIGHT: Under the rafters in a top-floor loft, a whirlpool tub provides soothing respite from stress. The mix of wood, tumbled limestone tile, and an antique bench give the room a Tuscan-farmhouse look.

ABOVE: A handcrafted copper, brass, and steel mirror, satin-finish brass faucet, painted porcelain sink, and an earth-tone tile countertop bring an Old World touch of color and pattern to this log-home bathroom.

Outfitting the Bath

The products you select to outfit your new bathroom will have an impact on the design and the budget. If your choose top-of-the-line products, expect a top-of-the-line bill. Factors that influence the cost of new fixtures, cabinetry, countertops, and flooring include updated technology, color, and type of finish. The "smarter" the device, the more you'll pay for it. Likewise, the fancier the finish, the higher the price tag. But cost does not always reflect quality, nor will it always bring satisfaction. Quality and personal comfort are the most important factors to consider when making any product selection.

Tubs. The possibilities are vast: soakers, whirlpools, classic claw-footed models, contoured shapes, ovals, or squares, freestanding, or set into a platform. It's your choice. Before buying, think about your bathing preferences. Do you prefer a long lingering soak or an invigorating hydromassage?

The classic claw-foot tub is popular with log-cabin owners because of its nostalgic appearance. You can find originals at salvage companies and refinish them to look like new. But every major plumbing manufacturer has at least one reproduction claw-foot tub in their lines, usually in a choice of colors.

Many builders prefer setting a tub in a platform or surround. Usually built of wood or covered with tile, these surrounds present a neat built-in look while concealing lines of plumbing that would normally be routed under the floor. Unlike many conventional frame homes, in most log homes, there isn't space to run pipes and wiring between floors. Tubs and toilets that are installed on raised platforms have the room needed to route pipes.

For freestanding bathtubs (as well as lavatories and toilets), contractors will use the interior framed walls to conceal vertical runs of plumbing or wire from one floor to another.

Showers. If two or more family members are sharing a bathroom, a separate shower unit is always a practical choice. Custom-built showers are typically constructed of solid-surfacing material, ceramic tile, stone, or concrete. Top-of-the-line features include massaging hydrotherapy sprays, steam units, a foot whirlpool, built-in seating and storage, or even media equipment.

Furniture-inspired cabinets, luxurious stone tiles, limestone counters, and bronze faucets juxtaposed with rustic log walls create a look of easy elegance.

OPPOSITE: This handsome bath features log walls softened by plaid wallpaper, an antique mirror, and lavatory with a thick granite counter.

BELOW: Earth-toned stone tiles in a matte finish surround this artfully detailed, hammered-copper sink. The vanity is framed in painted wood with fabric-paneled doors.

Amazing technology lets you enjoy a full body massage on a miserly amount of water. Although by law new showerheads may not deliver more than 2.5 gallons of water per minute, you can install as many as you wish.

You can also find prefabricated models that come as basic showers or extremely luxurious units that are fully loaded with exotic bells and whistles, such as multiple shower heads, steam, air and water jets, water towers, and gentle rain showers.

Depending on the size of your guest bath, you can save on space by installing a shower unit, instead of a separate or combination tub and shower.

Toilets. Believe it or not, you do have choices when selecting a toilet for your bathroom. Vitreous china is still the material of choice, but there's a wide range of colors and style options to suit different preferences.

Lavatories. You may find it difficult to select one lav over another because they come in so many materials, sizes, shapes, styles, and colors. Sculpted bowls and durable finishes can make this vessel a work of art—and an important element in your overall design, whether it's a freestanding pedestal or a bowl that is mounted above or below the counter.

Surfaces

Even in a well-ventilated bathroom, steam and moisture take their toll. So it is important to select materials for the walls, floors, vanity, and countertop that can hold up to moisture. Unless cost is a factor, steer away from plastic laminate and vinyl and choose a material that is more in keeping with the traditional log-home aesthetic. A natural-looking ceramic or glass tile, solid-surfacing material, wood, a natural stone—such as slate, granite, and concrete—will only enhance the look of handcraftsmanship that is intrinsic in a log home.

Ceramic Tile. Besides its practical attributes, such as durability, easy maintenance, and imperviousness to water, ceramic tile offers the greatest opportunity for bringing style and personality to your

bathroom. Use tile to add color, pattern, and texture to walls, floors, or countertops. It comes in a variety of sizes, shapes, and finishes. Visit a tile showroom in your area or the design department of a nearby home center to get ideas.

Solid-Surfacing Material. An extremely durable, easily maintained synthetic made of polyester or acrylic, solid-surfacing material is used to fabricate countertops, sinks, shower enclosures, and floors. It's not cheap, costing almost as much per linear foot as granite, but it wears long and well. It is completely impervious to water, and dents or abrasions can be repaired with a light sanding.

Wood. Log-home owners, who are known for their love of wood, may want to continue to use it throughout the room including the floor and countertops. If that's the case, wood must be properly sealed because of its susceptibility to water damage. A urethane or resin finish is recommended to protect it from mildew and warping. Certain types of wood, such teak, hold up better than other softer woods, such as pine.

Stone and Concrete. Granite, slate, and limestone are probably the most expensive materials you can choose for a countertop. Extremely durable, they also offer a rich, yet rustic, look to a cabin interior. Two other stone materials, limestone and concrete, are finding their way into the creative hands of today's designers. Unlike granite and slate, limestone has a more primitive, textured appeal. Concrete offers a wide range of design possibilities. It can be colored, shaped, carved, and inlaid with objects, such as tile, glass, shells, wood, or just about anything.

As a countertop, any one of these materials can introduce a dramatic element to the room. The only thing you have to be concerned about is making sure your

natural countertop is sealed to prevent cracking, staining, and mildew.

All of these materials are heavy, so beware if you plan to use them to fabricate a tub or shower, especially on the upper floor of the house. Check with your builder or contractor to find out if you will need to adjust the building plan to include additional support under the floor to carry the weight.

When you're considering stone, tile, or concrete for flooring, however, remember that they are cold underfoot, and unforgiving—any delicate object dropped on a stone or concrete surface will break. Install radiant in-floor heating to keep your toes warm. Stone or tile flooring may also pose a safety hazard if it becomes slick when wet. If you use one of these materials, choose a matte finish and slip-resistant rugs to prevent falls.

ABOVE: A long vanity with a brown marble top and copper sink sets the tone for this powder room's earthy atmosphere.

OPPOSITE: Built-in closets are great for storing linens and bath accessories. Here, light-colored louver doors blend with the wood-paneled walls.

Bathroom Storage

Undoubtedly, an important aspect of your new home's bath design is storage. To serve all bathing and grooming needs, each bathroom will need space for extra linens, a clothes hamper, and cleaning supplies. You may even want to include storage for exercise equipment, magazines, and CDs, especially if you plan to use the room as a retreat for quiet time after a day at work.

Ask yourself whether one vanity is sufficient. How many people will share it? Do you require a medicine cabinet? How about a linen closet? Think about the way the bathrooms will be used. For example, will small children need storage for bath toys? Ideally, that should be some place other than along the ledge of the tub. If you don't want to tote dirty clothes to a downstairs laundry room, plan enough space for a closet to house a compact washer and dryer. These are just a few of the storage-related issues to discuss with your designer.

LIGHTING

In a bathroom that is less than 100 square feet, one light fixture is sufficient. Install another fixture for each additional 50 square feet. For efficiency and comfort while grooming, task lighting will be much appreciated by family members and guests in the area of the sink. Avoid placing a light fixture overhead where a person will stand when looking in a mirror. A light source that is directly above your head will cast unflattering shadows on your face, especially around your eyes and under the nose. Designers suggest that mounting a light strip or a single fixture on the wall above the mirror is okay because the position of the light source will be in front of your face rather than above it. Lighting the shower or tub area is a good idea, too. Make sure the fixture is specifically for installation in a wet area.

EXTRA DETAILS

- If you have any leeway in your plan, place the toilet in an enclosed area of the bathroom so that it is not visible to the rest of the space.
- Add a linen closet or an armoire for storage.
- Plan for separate tub and shower areas and a double sink. This will prevent traffic jams in a shared space.
- Install a towel warmer.
- Include wiring for a TV and a speaker system.
- Consider adding a book or magazine rack.

Personal Retreats

In this busy world, everyone needs a private getaway. The most obvious choice for this in many homes is the master bedroom. That is where you go for a short nap on a Sunday afternoon, or to sit back and snatch a few hours enjoying a favorite book or catching up on a stack of magazines. Because most other rooms in the house are used as communal spaces, your bedroom can sometimes be the only place to escape.

Winding down after a stressful day is not always easy, but you can create a serene atmosphere with soothing color schemes, furnishings, and decoration. What makes a bedroom relaxing?

Start with comfortable bedding, namely a good mattress. Don't skimp on this. A high-quality mattress will ensure restful sleeping and can prevent morning backaches. Another factor is thoughtful lighting. It should suit the mood of the room and be adequate for reading, dressing, relaxing, or watching TV.

Last but not least is quiet—after all this is your retreat. You don't have to completely soundproof the bedroom, however. Fortunately, having thick log walls is a good start. Solid-wood doors, double-pane windows, and thick wall-to-wall carpeting or rugs will also contribute to the over all quietude in your room.

A Room With A View

Increase the luxury of your private space by adding a balcony or patio to your plan. Looking out on a magnificent view is a wonderful way to kick back and relax.

The addition of glass doors leading to the outside will also break up the expanse of log walls and fill the bedroom with generous natural sunlight. If you prefer not to be awakened at the first light of day, install room-darkening shades, louvered shutters, blinds, or lined curtains.

Style-Wise

Unlike other rooms, the bedroom is not a multipurpose space. In order to create a retreat you have to avoid giving in to the idea of using one corner of the room as a home office. Taking any type of work into the bedroom is not conducive to rest.

If the master bedroom is shared, decide together whether or not to include a TV. If you like to watch movies or listen to music in bed, indulge yourself, but keep electronics out of view when you're not using them by concealing them in an entertainment center. Be aware, however, that most sleep experts recommend leaving the TV out of the bedroom for a better sleep.

Draw your color scheme from the palette you've chosen for one of the other rooms in the house, or pick colors from the

view outside of your window. If you are a morning person and have the time to luxuriate in the bedroom until later, consider warm, invigorating colors. Or if you want your evening retreat to soothe away the cares of the day, pick from the cooler hues.

The master bedroom in a log home generally conforms to the style chosen for the main rooms of the house, except for the choice in flooring. If you love something soft and warm under your feet, this is one room in a log cabin where it is, aesthetically speaking, okay to use a plush carpet.

Furniture

The single decorative focus in most bedrooms is the bed. You can have anything from a rustic four-poster timber piece, to a simple upholstered headboard. Dress it up

OPPOSITE: French doors open onto a balcony. The simple furnishings in this room create a low-key atmosphere conducive to relaxation.

ABOVE: Framed by light, bleached log walls, and the mission-style furnishings combine with the rattan sofa to create a comfortable environment.

RIGHT: Leopard-print carpeting lends an exotic touch to this traditional-style room that features an antique reproduction four-poster bed.

THINK OUTSIDE THE BEDROOM

Break the rules and install a small kitchenette behind closed doors. Include a sink, coffeemaker, and compact refrigerator so you won't have to run to the kitchen for a snack or a cold beverage when you want it.

OPPOSITE: This relaxing bedroom has a queen-size bed with a rustic log headboard, a private balcony, and a fireplace with a TV cabinet overhead.

RIGHT: Located in an old log cabin, this master bedroom is decorated in the American Country style in keeping with its pioneer roots.

BOTTOM RIGHT: Curtains add softness to the wood walls in this guest bedroom. The blue patchwork quilt on the bed coordinates with the window treatment.

with attractive linens and pillows that can be changed with the seasons. Get creative by fashioning a headboard out of a wrought-iron gate, a rustic ladder, or just hang a large tapestry or Native American blanket on the wall behind the bed.

In a room where two people are often waking up and getting dressed at the same time, it's a good idea to include separate storage areas for each one. Plan on having a dresser and bureau, two closets, and twin nightstands. If your budget permits, add two dressing rooms between the master bedroom and bath.

Log cabins are, by nature, eclectic. When it comes to furniture, mix it up; buy interesting individual pieces instead of an all-matching suite. A twig end table, a rag rug, and an Adirondack-style chest of drawers will create the feeling that the room has evolved over time, settling into an unobtrusive style that looks uncontrived. Include your favorite collectibles and antiques; throw in a bookcase and an old blanket chest. Create a quiet spot for reading and relaxing with a comfortable chair and ottoman, chaise, or a recliner, along with a small table and lamp. Consider installing a small fireplace or pellet stove in the room so that you can sit and relax by the fire. The whole effect can be simple but not spare, carefully thought out with a seemingly casual look. Mix objects that relate to your life rather than a duplicating a furniture showroom or page from a catalog.

5

Outdoor Views

ften, one of the most appealing aspects of living in a log home is its beautiful natural setting. If you want the surrounding landscape to play a pivotal role in the overall feel of your log home, consider factors such as the position of the house on the site, the types of trees and shrubbery that will be present, and the position of the driveway, walks, patios, and decks. Of course, always keep in mind the direction of the sun and the surrounding views.

With a Plan in Mind

To design anything, you must gather all the elements you'd like to include and then put them together in a coherent way. Builders and landscapers agree that the project moves faster when clients have a good sense of how they want their property to look outside as well as inside. Gathering ideas as early as possible in the design process and keeping a separate folder of outdoor living spaces, inspirational garden layouts, and storage facilities can make decision making much easier. Look at readily available sources, such as the Internet and garden books.

You could also drive through the surrounding area to see how other log-home owners have handled exterior design. Or consult a professional, such as a landscape architect or landscape designer. Ask for photos of their recent projects. The more you see, the more you will learn and apply to your own dream project.

The landscape design should provide a framework for your outdoor living space. The views, sight lines, property configuration, and family lifestyle and traffic patterns must work together. Spend ample time getting acquainted with your site and note its characteristics and any special features. What are the site's assets? Are there extraordinary vantage points or natural elements, such as a lake or stream? Instead of cutting down a handsome vintage tree, will it be possible to build around it?

Allow the land to frame the house, not overwhelm it. The location of trees can be a crucial factor in your exterior design. Too many will visually compete with the logs. On the other hand, well-placed trees can act as a shade arbor offering respite from the summer heat. For a log home, the best site designs are those that begin and end with simplicity as their guiding principle because the structure itself makes such a strong statement.

Blending in

No outdoor living space is completely successful unless it is integrated with the surrounding landscape. Careful planning of the site and choosing the placement of the

OPPOSITE: The location of trees and any water views are important factors to consider before deciding on the placement of porches and decks.

LEFT: Instead of a column, a large tree trunk complete with a whimsical family of carved bears holds up a corner of this front porch.

This prow-style home features a wraparound deck that incorporates a corner gazebo, opening the exterior to magnificent seasonal views of the surrounding woodland.

A covered entrance featuring full-log columns shelters this porch. The handcrafted stone base blends into the landscape and protects the deck from water damage.

plantings are crucial decisions. Before designing any areas, think about the kinds of activities you anticipate enjoying outdoors. How much time will you spend eating and entertaining on a deck or patio? Do you need outdoor space where you can relax in peace and quiet?

Because a deck, patio, or porch is usually used more often as a fair-weather family room, comfortable seating comes first—arranged for conversation, as it would be in an indoor room. Add to this an area for snacking or outdoor cooking and other recreation. Consider also the ages of your family members and other factors that will define your needs. Remember that these are outdoor rooms; the more components that can remain in place in inclement weather, the easier and more inviting it will

be to use the space. Decide whether you need shaded areas, or those exposed to the sun. Where you position your outdoor rooms in relation to the house, trees, or other buildings will determine how much sun or shade they get. Awnings, umbrellas, and pergolas can be used as protection from the sun on decks or patios. If your home is in a warm climate most of the year, you can get more use out of the decks and porches by screening in one or two. Screens can turn a porch into an extra bedroom during the summer.

One more note: on the exterior of the house, your choice of materials and colors can creatively reflect your personality as well as the homes's relationship to its site. Decide whether the exterior will blend into or contrast with its surroundings.

Landscape Design

Landscaping is more than just the garden and placement of outdoor living areas. It can also include grading, drainage, water features, walls, and walks, boulder placement, outdoor kitchens, and heated driveways. Like an interior designer, a landscape professional can help you create pleasing outdoor living spaces, taking advantage of the existing foliage around the house, arranging garden paths, and coordinating plants and flowers. In addition, a landscape architect or designer can provide ideas for hardscaping with structural elements, such as a gazebo, pergola, arbor, and fencing.

Certain principles of gardening apply especially to log homes. Try not to plant too close to the house or you will be watering your walls while watering the plants. Logs are sensitive to excess moisture, causing degeneration of the wood.

You might also consider adding a stone walkway to the house. It can be simple or elaborate in form and color. Colored pavers allow more creativity with patterns and hues. But walkways can also blend with the landscape for a subtle scheme.

Costs

Mistakes in exterior design can be expensive, so let a professional guide you through this rough terrain. Plan to set aside at least 5 to 7 percent of your resources for landscaping. (Some custom-designed landscapes can consume as much as 12 to 14 percent of the total budget.) Many homeowners get so caught up in the building and decorating of the house that they end up with little or nothing left to spend on the exterior spaces. Be prepared for this facet of the building project by setting aside a realistic allowance of funds.

Also, think of upkeep before you decide on a sprawling lawn, luxurious shrub borders, and colorful flower beds. Designing a beautiful garden is one thing, maintaining it is another matter. Depending on how much and what you plant, gardens can be a time-consuming hobby in the long run. Alternatively there are low-maintenance plantings available for the casual gardener.

RIGHT: A paved walkway blends with the surrounding boulders that dot the landscape as well as the river rocks on the home's foundation.

OPPOSITE: Echoing the colors and texture of the surrounding walls, this side garden is decorated with natural stone, wood, and folk art.

Blending Indoor and Outdoor Spaces

Any attached or adjacent outdoor space that provides total or partial shelter can be designed as an extension of your home's interior living area. In fact, outdoor "rooms" should be as enjoyable as those inside your house. When you're planning these outdoor areas, use all of the same guidelines that apply to interior design. Aim for comfort and style and a natural flow between indoors and outdoors. This is especially appropriate to log homes, where the boundaries between the indoors and nature is often blurred.

Developing your outdoor living space can also give the interiors of your home an added dimension. Study the floor plan of the house with your designer. Where can you create garden views that can also be enjoyed from the inside? Can a patio or deck serve as an extension of the master suite or great room? A deck or patio at floor level with the great room complete with a garden view will not only make the room appear larger, but so much more attractive as well.

Design the garden so that the view from inside is alluring. Incorporating transitional space—a porch, patio, or deck—between the building and the landscape creates a link between the two areas. Coordinate colors, choosing plantings that extend your interior palette. Sometimes the simplest plan can be the most effective—a straight paved path leading to a focal point, such as a tall garden urn or water feature are perfect examples.

The wraparound windows on this enclosed porch expose a sweeping view of the landscape, turning it into a visual extension of the space.

Water Features

However large or small, a water feature, such as a fountain or pond, will create a soothing focal point in your outdoor living area. The location and size of a pond will be restricted by the space available but its shape and style are limited only by your imagination. A pond or any moving water feature doesn't have to be confined to the back of the house, either. Placing it in a front patio or entryway can be a refreshing place to pause on the way into the house.

Small ponds and reflecting pools may be permanent structures with brick or poured-concrete bases. Pools and ponds can also be made with either rigid or flexible liners. They can be custom or built from kits. Stones around the edge of the liners keep them in place and add a more natural look. To prevent algae growth, water must be kept aerated so you will need a pump. A power source will be needed for this and a ground-fault circuit interrupter (GFCI) to prevent possible electrocution should water and electricity meet. Ask your landscaper about the cost of designing a pond. If you prefer to do it yourself, you can find kits or all of the materials, including flexible pond liners, at your local home center.

Exterior Decorating

Because your log home is bound to make a strong visual impact on the surrounding landscape, it's a good idea to design your outdoor areas to coordinate with the architecture. For a warm, decorative touch, try adding recycled objects to the garden: an old park bench; ancient farm equipment; or flowers and herbs planted in antique barrels and boxes. Bring your personality to the garden area with the addition of your favorite accessories, such as a birdbath carved out of stone, a glowing copper lantern, melodic wind chimes, a sundial, or a collection of folk art birdhouses.

ABOVE: To achieve a balance in the landscape, outbuildings, such as this log-style garage, should be designed to reflect the look of the main house.

LEFT: The design of this log-home development and its magnificent landscape is reminiscent of the classic form of ancient Japanese architecture.

Rustic twig-style furniture is at home on this deck overlooking the mountains. Soft cushions add comfort to the natural rush seats. For added color, the homeowners planted flowers in a barrel-style container.

Furnishings for your garden, patio, or deck will probably include comfortable, durable, and versatile seating. You'll also need adequate surfaces for preparing and serving meals and convenient placement of a grill and storage. If you intend to use your outdoor area at night, create a plan with your designer that includes outdoor lighting, heaters, and a fireplace or fire pit.

Furniture

As you would with indoor furniture, choose pieces that will suit the scale and size of your outdoor rooms. Massive furnishings will overpower a small patio and delicate twig furniture will get lost on a large deck. Another pitfall is to use too much furniture. Whenever possible, choose pieces that are multifunctional so that a bench can store cushions, for example. Look for chairs that will adjust from sitting to lounging positions.

When placing furniture on your deck or patio, consider function, typical traffic patterns, and views that you want to highlight or hide. If your deck is small, use items such as benches to define pathways. Try to place dining sets for small gatherings in areas where there is no through-traffic to avoid guests having to shift their chairs every time someone passes. Place the dining table where it will be easily accessible for both indoor and outdoor food preparation. For large gatherings, design your outdoor room with several, rather than one, large sitting area. The secondary dining spots should be big enough for chairs and small tables to hold food and drinks.

OUTDOOR KITCHENS

Decks and patios are often used for grilling more than anything else. Even during the winter season, many families enjoy cooking outside. Whether you choose a portable or permanent grill, you may want to add a food preparation and staging counter nearby. Include a counter with a cabinet for basic cooking and serving supplies.

If your budget allows, you might install a fully equipped outdoor kitchen with separate food preparation, dining, and storage areas. Some of the most elaborate designs feature granite counters, cabinets, sinks, full-size cooktops, refrigerators, and freezers that have been designed for outdoor use.

Do you like to watch the game while you're partying outdoors? How about a DVD after dinner? Manufacturers are now bringing high-definition TVs, DVDs, and surround sound to outdoor rooms all over the country. So if you've got the cash, get ready to watch your favorite show or movie under the stars.

Decks, Porches, and Patios

Decks are a great way to add square footage to your home and maximize available outdoor space. The naturally rustic look of a wood deck is especially attractive when merged with a log home. A deck can also incorporate natural elements, such as a large tree or rocks, or it can be designed to gracefully merge with the architecture of your log home. The addition of a grill, table and chairs, and a fireplace will turn the space into a great outdoor eating area. Again, it is important to think ahead about your lifestyle as you plan the deck.

Rather than investing in interior space that you may only use on special occasions, situating your main deck off the great room will allow the two areas to flow together. Your house will then be able to accommodate large gatherings without the expense of additional interior square footage. Planning square footage based on actual use can save you money that can be best spent in other areas.

Choosing the right site for your deck may seem obvious. Nevertheless, it's worth thinking all of the possibilities. For example, where are the best views? For a deck used to cook and serve meals, connecting to the indoor kitchen seems logical. Possible locations for elevated decks include outside the bedrooms, home office, and library. Assuming you have more than one option, exposure to the sun may be the final deciding factor. A south-facing deck will receive sun almost all day. East- and west-facing decks get sun in the morning and afternoon, respectively. Southeast or southwest-facing decks will receive the sun for longer periods than decks that face due east or west. However, north-facing decks, unless they extend beyond the shadow of the house, will receive little or no sun for much of the day.

If you are envisioning having an expansive view from your deck, situate it higher than the first floor. A deck that is adjacent to the second or third floor of the house is best for this. Placing it on a lower floor will give you a better view of your garden.

Natural Assets

When you're building any type of house, rough, steep, or uneven terrain can be a liability. However, you and your builder may be able to turn this liability into an advantage. A moderately sloping site could be a natural for a multilevel deck that steps down (or up) the incline. Large rock outcroppings or boulders can provide natural focal points for your deck and can also be considered an asset when worked into the overall design.

Porches

One of the most maintenance-friendly types of outdoor spaces, a porch can also shelter you from the sun, rain, and snow while protecting your logs from inclement weather. Adding screens to a porch is an easy way to let you enjoy your outdoor room even during the peak seasons for pesky insects. If you prefer the look of an open area, you can also cover just a portion of your porch. You can even double up on bedroom space by creating a screened-in sleeping area on the porch during the warm weather.

Quite often, log-home porches will span the length of the front of the house, but this is not the only option. Depending on the building's layout, the other possibility would be to install a small front porch as an entryway, a place to stand out of the rain or snow while looking for your keys. Log-home owners are also requesting wider front porches: 6 to 8 feet rather than the standard 3 to 4 feet. This wider version can accommodate more furnishings, including a porch swing. Simple additions, such as potted plants, hanging baskets, and window boxes, will also add a nice touch of color and texture to an all-wood porch.

The key consideration for any porch is that it complies with the architectural style of the house. It needs to be consistent in detail, scale, and character with the rest of the structure and not give the impression that it was tacked on as an afterthought. An attractive porch will not only provide a relaxing place to hang out, but can also enhance your house's curb appeal and add to its personality.

Patios

Landscape designers have referred to the patio as an exterior living room with a hard floor and no roof. Often attached to the house, a patio can be located on the side, back, or even in the middle of the structure. The patio's exact location will depend on the size and location of your house, as well as how you intend to use it. You might want to build one near the kitchen so that food can be easily brought in and out, or position a private patio off the master bedroom, creating a quiet place for relaxing. The beauty of a patio is that, unlike the more architecturally structured porch or a deck, it can be designed to gently harmonize with the surrounding landscape. The

OPPOSITE TOP: Furnishings on this porch echo the rustic style of the building. An Adirondack-style swing placed at one end of the room draws your eye across the length of the space.

OPPOSITE BOTTOM: The walkway connecting the deck and gazebo can also double as a porch. A platform extension with room for a picnic table provides access from the deck to the yard.

LEFT: A screened-in porch, dressed with potted plants, wraps around the corner of the house to accommodate an additional entrance to the home.

two areas can naturally flow into each other. The unifying link between the patio and the surrounding land depends on your choice of surface material, edging, and walkways that join the patio to the garden. It's all about choosing the colors and materials that will create a natural transition between the house and the land. Your local garden center can help with choosing the appropriate materials, as well as provide a great resource for design ideas. Popular choices for log homes are interlocking stone or concrete pavers because of their natural coloring and rough texture.

As with any outdoor room, think about how its use will bring you the most enjoyment for your leisure time. Evaluate your site's assets and liabilities, and again call in the experts to decide on the right location. Consider having the most advantageous view, which could be anything from a distant mountaintop to a flower-filled garden bed.

VERANDAS

A veranda, popular in the South and Southwest, is a cross between a porch and a patio. Attached to the side of the house, the veranda consists of a ground floor roofed platform with supporting columns. This type of architecture not only provides a shaded area for sitting but also protects the log walls and windows from direct sunlight, fading the logs and heating up the interior of the house. Because it is on ground level, the veranda, like a patio, provides a perfect addition for enjoyment of the garden and outdoor living.

BELOW: Overhead spotlights, located under the eaves, are used to spread light across the exterior of this home, while creating a warm glow against the snow-covered landscape.

BOTTOM: Lighting placed in the rafters of this log-home entry looks dramatic and defines the structure's magnificent architectural features.

OPPOSITE: Decorative lighting highlights the architectural features of this home and garden. Adding lighting to the yard will also enhance the view from the deck at night.

Outdoor Lighting

Ground-fault circuit interrupters (GFCIs), built-in lighting, and ceiling fans can make all the difference for nighttime use of decks, porches, and patios. Lighting defines spaces at night. It is also a necessary factor for safety. Both on-deck and inground low-voltage systems are good ideas. Although lighting systems can be intricate, and sometimes costly, they are worth the price you pay as protection against tripping and falling in the dark. Features may include fixtures for aesthetic highlighting of plantings or other yard features, as well as timed sequencing that turns on and off automatically or when triggered by motion.

When you're devising an outdoor plan, illuminating all of the entrances should be your first priority. Wall-mounted fixtures, such as sconces or lanterns, are available in a wide variety of styles and finishes, so you should be able to find ones that coordinate with your home's architecture and exterior hardware. Supplement wall-mounted lamps with recessed fixtures in any soffit that overhangs your deck. Besides offering excellent general illumination, recessed lights will also accent the beauty of your logs at night.

The next important step is to light the transition into your yard. Low-voltage lighting is a good choice here. Wiring for low-voltage systems is fairly simple. Use

TYPES OF LIGHTS

Outdoor decorative lighting fixtures are available in both line and low voltages and often with a choice of lamps, including incandescent, halogen, and compact fluorescent. The latter are energy efficient and long lasting.

path-lighting fixtures near the foot of stairs, as well as lights you can recess into the stair risers.

Decorative lighting can be used to set a mood on your deck, porch, or patio. The possibilities are endless, from low-voltage commercial string lights to fixtures that hide in your planters. Lighting your yard will not only enhance your outdoor areas, it can also add a little drama while making you feel more secure. Check out your local home and garden center or the Internet. You'll find so many possibilities from which to choose, including uplights and spotlights (usually used to accent trees and sculpture); spread lights for throwing light horizontally across a garden; and lights for revealing texture on surfaces. Your builder will probably also have suggestions for a basic lighting plan or consider hiring a lighting designer. Inquire if your landscape designer includes lighting design as part of his or her services.

Store It

If your log home will be the center of activities for the whole family, complete with kayaks, bicycles, skis, fishing gear, and gardening supplies, look into including outdoor storage facilities rather than taking up space inside the house. You can have a small matching log shed made or buy an inexpensive storage shed that will accommodate boats, snowmobiles, and other gear.

Apply the same storage principles used inside your home to the outdoors to create

SMART IDEA

Don't let garbage cans and recycling bins intrude on your landscape. Build a log-style locker to keep them out of sight and out of reach of raccoons and other uninvited wildlife.

This porch's cozy seating area, complete with a large river-stone wood-burning fireplace, rivals many interior living rooms for charm and comfort.

a serene, clutter-free personal paradise. Solutions will differ according to the size of your lot and the amount of stuff that needs stowing. From a simple deck bench with a lid that opens to store pads and pillows for the patio furniture, to a freestanding storehouse that's been custom made to match your log home, there are many ways to keep your exterior accessories orderly and accessible.

Whether custom-constructed or ready-made, your storage shed should be neat and well organized. Carefully plan the interior spaces to suit your goals. If the shed must meet several storage needs, section off or zone the inside with one wall or area, perhaps designated for sports gear and toys, another for garden and lawn care, and another for party or pool supplies.

FLOORING OPTIONS

Exterior flooring is subjected to even more abuse than roofing because of its exposure to the combination of foot traffic and the elements. This is why it is so important to invest in high-quality materials. When it comes to choosing materials for decks and porches, there are more options available than ever before in both natural and synthetic woods. Most new products have one thing in common: they are all aimed at producing deck and porch flooring that requires less maintenance.

Redwood, cedar, and cypress are the three most commonly used types of untreated wood for outdoor flooring:

• **Redwood** ranges in color from light to dark red and has a handsome straight grain that takes finishes well. Heartwood redwood is resistant to rot, decay, and insects. The drawback is the price. It is often four times the cost of pressure-treated wood.

• **Cedar** (typically western red cedar) has many of the same qualities as redwood but costs significantly less. For a rustic look you can choose a knotty grade. Like redwood, cedar takes finishes better than heavier woods, such as southern yellow pine.

• **Bald cypress** is less well known except in its native regions—the American Southeast for instance. The trees flourish in swampy areas, hence the wood's natural resistance to rot and insects (heartwood only). Prices vary, depending on how far you live from the cypress's point of origin.

Many homeowners prefer to work with pressure-treated lumber because it is a most cost effective and practical outdoor material. Available species include pine, hemlock, and fir. The most popular are southern pine and Douglas fir. Extremely resistant to rot and insect damage, the wood is processed in a vacuum chamber and filled with a liquid preservative. The process of treating the wood with arsenic has been replaced with environmentally safe copper compounds.

Because of cosmetic improvements over the last few years, synthetic materials have grown in popularity among log-home owners. These products, also known as composites, combine wood fiber and plastics, often reclaimed from wood waste and recycled plastics. Although synthetics still don't quite look or feel like wood, they do have several advantages over the real thing: they will not rot or splinter; they come pre-colored so they don't need finishing; and depending on the type of the material, they can be formed into sweeping curves on a deck. The big selling point is the fact that it requires less maintenance than wood. On the other hand, synthetic lumber products are expensive—often more so than top-quality wood products. They also get dirty, can stain and scratch, and some will support the growth of mold and mildew.

6

Everlasting Beauty

fter its construction, your log home will have to be protected from the natural elements that can seriously threaten its good looks and structural integrity. The beauty and longevity of the logs will depend on the level of protection you provide. Taking steps to preserve the wood exterior with proper initial treatment, regular inspections, and routine maintenance is a wise course. Here's what you need to know to ensure the lasting beauty of your log home in a way that is safe for your family.

Caring for Log Surfaces

According to Joan Decker, sales consultant with Beaver Mountain Log and Cedar Homes in Hancock, New York, some wood species, such as northeastern white pine and western red cedar are "moderately to highly resistant to rot, which is not to say they won't need to be treated later. Because one side of the logs will be the interior wall, it's important to avoid adversely affecting the living environment with chemicals. Rather than pretreating entire logs at the factory with chemicals or other toxic compounds that can infiltrate the lungs, we provide an exterior wood preservative and water-repellent finish blended with a mild pesticide. This finish is applied to the exterior of the home after the shell is erected."

Protecting your wood exterior will also allow stains and preservatives to absorb into the wood fully and evenly.

Logs arriving from the manufacturer may have a "mill-glaze" finish. This happens when the mill's blades cut the wood—the tree's water-soluble resins rise to the surface, leaving a hard varnish-like glaze. Because mill glaze will interfere with the log's ability to bond with a finish, it is important to remove the glaze before attempting to apply a stain or protective finish to the wood. The best way to remove mill glaze is with a light sanding.

Before starting to finish and stain the logs, ask your builder to perform color and

ABOVE: Clear finishes are a popular choice for log interiors. They not only protect the wood from moisture and dirt but also allow the beauty of the grain to show.

OPPOSITE: The full-log rafters, wood flooring, and paneled walls shown here are covered in a light, natural finish that gives the room a warm, spacious look.

batch tests on a sample log to see how the final color will look. Finishing products are based on the species of wood, the soil conditions surrounding your home (such as the moisture content and what types of insects are present), and the area of the country where you live. Log manufacturers will steer you to the best product for your home. They usually recommend using the same brand for each application. Using a variety of preservative and stain products can result in adherence problems later.

Preserve and Seal

Once the logs are dry, they have to be protected. The first step requires the application of the preservative. One of the most widely used is a borate solution that acts as a fungicide and a deterrent to decay. It is also an insecticide that is proven to be deadly to termites, powder post beetles, and carpenter ants, while not harmful to humans, animals, or the environment. The preservative is usually applied by brush or spray and penetrates the wood where it crystallizes and protects it from destructive organisms. After this treatment, a stain can be applied to the exterior surfaces of the house.

Utimately, the best protection against decay, however, is to keep the walls dry. For this reason, all exterior wood surfaces should be coated with a water-repellent finish. Make sure to apply a premium product that will permit the wood to breathe, allowing moisture to escape.

That is important because logs can develop cracks due to moisture making its way out of the wood. These cracks are natural and do not impair the structural integrity of the log, but can cause a problem if the crack is set in a direction that holds water. Exterior cracks that retain moisture need to be sealed with caulk or chinking before finishing.

LEFT: Strong sunlight can cause serious ultraviolet damage to log walls. Adding a light tint to the finish will protect the logs from fading over time.

BELOW: Protect the exterior wood surfaces with both a preservative and a water-repellent finish that will allow the logs to breathe and moisture to escape.

HOW TO CLEAN LOGS

Working in small sections, start from the bottom and work up, wetting the wood with water. (This will prevent streaking.) Once the wood is wet, generously apply a solution of 4 ounces of trisodium phosphate (TSP), 3 quarts of water, and 1 quart of bleach using a garden-pump sprayer, again starting at the bottom. Scrub the surface using a stiff nylon brush for 15 to 20 minutes. Do not let the solution dry. After you have wet one side of the house, wash the surface to remove the solution. If you use a power washer (some experts advise against power washing logs), keep the nozzle about 1 foot from the surface. In addition, make sure the pressure does not exceed 500 psi to prevent damaging the logs. Allow for at least three non-humid days for drying before adding any surface application. If the surface is not completely dry before finishing, moisture will try to escape and cause the wood to blister.

Most homeowners stain the logs before applying a sealant. Staining enhances the natural highlights of the wood and prevents ultraviolet (UV) rays from drying out the wood's fibers.

The final step in preserving the wood is finishing it with a sealant. If you decide to skip the staining process and just apply a sealant, keep in mind that you will still have to add a tint or color of some sort to the clear finish for adequate UV protection. Applying a clear finish to the wood without adding color will still protect it from mold, mildew, and insects, but expect the wood to turn gray over time.

Adding the topcoat is a very important final step that will not only protect your logs from water, dirt, and grime, but it will also lighten your list of annual maintenance chores. Make sure to give special attention to log ends that are exposed. This is a vulnerable area on log homes and a favorite entryway for insects. Check to see that they are properly sealed.

Never varnish or paint the exterior of your log home. Oil-based paint products will seal the wood and prevent it from breathing. Varnish and paint finishes are not designed to withstand the expansion and contraction of the wood fibers caused by changes in temperature and humidity, which can make the finish crack or peel.

PROTECTING YOUR LOG HOME

A serious problem associated with log homes is decay, which can be caused by splash back from faulty gutters or inadequate eaves—exposing the logs to excessive moisture—unprotected log ends, and insect infestation. To prevent decay, make sure your home is designed to avoid situations that will overly expose it to the elements.

- Include wide roof overhangs of at least 18 to 24 inches on all sides of the house to help keep rain, snow, and sun away from the logs.

- For patio and terrace floors, use brick or stone rather than landscape timbers to avoid the need to replace weather-damaged logs.

- Use a drain tile system to gather roof water and direct it away from the house.

- To ensure proper drainage, make sure that the land slopes away from the log structure.

- Check to see if any of the wood surfaces are touching dirt anywhere around the house. Any wood making contact with the ground should be pressure-treated.

- Clean gutters and downspouts regularly to prevent water from backing up, and check for any leaks.

- Design porches and decks so that they slope away from the house and foundation, allowing excess water to drain.

Although wood protection represents a small portion of your overall expense, it is actually one of the most important elements in maintaining the longevity and beauty of your home. For information about cleaning exterior logs, see "How to Clean Logs," on page 133.

Interior log walls that have been treated with a nonporous finish are easy to dust and clean. In fact, you can use any product intended for wood floors to clean interior log walls. First wipe the surface with a clean rag to remove dust and loose dirt, or use the hose attachment of your vacuum cleaner. Then with a clean mop, wash the areas near the top of the walls. You can use a damp sponge to wipe the logs on the lower portion of the wall.

ABOVE: Applying a clear finish to wood will make it easier to clean the surfaces of dust and grime, especially in hard-to-reach areas, such as this small sleeping loft.

RIGHT: Using various tinted stains throughout the interior will not only enhance the surfaces but also provide the option of using a different color in each room.

7

Real Log-Home Living

Filled with the warmth and comfort that comes from living in a natural setting, some owners compare log-home living with being on vacation year-round. This chapter shows how individual log-home owners decorate their rooms with character and personal style, including a couple so smitten with the organic beauty of an alligator bark juniper tree found on their property that they made it the focal point of their great room.

Home on the Range

A simple, yet elegant, ranch scheme defines this western-style compound.

Southwest Montana, also known as "Gold West Country," is an area of the United States that offers a real feeling of the Old West. Fortuitously located near a national park, the area is home to miners, artists, outdoor enthusiasts, and a fair share of working ranches complete with horses, sheep, cows, and real cowboys.

Drawn to the scenic vistas of the nearby mountain range, the homeowners knew this would be the perfect place for a second home. After extensively exploring the region, they purchased a 10,000-acre ranch

that came with several outbuildings and an old square-hewn log schoolhouse. The original plans called for two new buildings, a large main house and smaller guest cabin. But all of that changed during the construction. "They were so pleased with the way the guest cabin turned out they decided not to go ahead with their plans for a bigger house," says architect Candace Tillotson-Miller of Tillotson-Miller Architects in Livingston, Montana, who, along with interior designers Charles Gandy and Bill Peace of Gandy/Peace,

The rustic look carries over into the kitchen with its breakfast bar made of hand-hewn logs. Countertops and cabinets are fashioned from Douglas fir with a rough-cut edge. Horizontal log beams are used to visually separate the kitchen from the great room.

Atlanta Georgia, and builder Chris Derham of Yellowstone Traditions, Bozeman, Montana, designed and renovated the three cabins that make up the family compound. Tillotson-Miller added, "The smaller-size cabin reflected a coziness that really appealed to them, so they decided to turn that into the main house and build a two-room bunkhouse for guests."

The one-room log schoolhouse, built at the turn of the twentieth century, was moved about a mile closer to the family compound near the river and converted into a fishing cabin, office, and retreat for the homeowners, as well as additional guest quarters. The fishing cabin, measuring 18x32 feet, has a sleeping loft space, a bath-

ABOVE: Rustic pine roots and logs were skillfully formed into a stairway banister and coat rack for the entrance hall in the main house. In the hands of a craftsman, this use of "random" timber becomes functional art.

BELOW: Bill Peace's and Charles Gandy's color scheme of earthy browns and golds was influenced by the natural colors that surround the property. The rooms have a laid-back look using a mix of recycled materials, antiques, and leather furnishings that reflect the home's original nineteenth-century ranch style.

RIGHT: The living room's focal point, a dramatic Harlowton Moss Rock fireplace, rises to a height of 20 ft., making the space appear larger. A collection of hats hangs high across the top of the windows.

The bunkhouse's glassed-in porch has two-over-two windows that easily convert to screens in the summer, making this room a favorite dining spot year-round.

room with washer/dryer, and kitchenette and is decorated in a rustic style similar to the main house.

The main house itself is made from standing dead timber—in this case, pole pine—which gives the logs an authentic "aged" look. The walls are actually built as a frame structure with vapor barriers, insulation, and a stud wall. This wall frame is covered on the interior and exterior with 2x6 split dead timber logs attached to the frame, similar to a veneer. This sandwich effect allows for the walls to look like solid logs inside and out, with the added benefit of having an insulated interior section.

Whenever possible, Tillotson-Miller used materials that were recycled from some of the ramshackle outbuildings on the property. These time-weathered materials contributed to the new building's warm traditional ranch look, resulting in a family compound that reflects the natural beauty of the land.

> "Pleased with the coziness of their smaller guest cabin, the homeowners decided to forgo plans for a large main house."

ABOVE: Rugged walls balance against the smooth Arts and Crafts-style cabinetry, giving the master bath an elegant spa-look within the log-cabin ambiance.

LEFT: Bringing the outside in, the bunkhouse features hand-crafted log bunk beds designed to look as if they are growing out of the floor.

OPPOSITE: In the guest room, furnishings are balanced between dressy and casual. The softness of white lace bed linens is juxtaposed with leather club chairs and burlap curtains, all framed by rough log walls.

Located in the main house, this screened-in porch is used for casual meals well into early winter. The porch's small stone fireplace was designed to create a cozy setting.

"The walls of the main house are covered in standing dead timber, giving the logs an authentic 'aged' log-cabin look."

ABOVE: The porch of the main house overlooks the mountain range. One of two new buildings, this house was carefully designed to blend with the original structures in the compound.

Brookbank Canyon Ranch

Powered by solar energy, an old ranch gets a new life.

While driving through the Arizona White Mountains in 1992, Lois and Jerry Jacka, a husband and wife writer/photographer team, came across an old ranch site on the Mogollon Rim in eastern Arizona. "It was love at first sight," says Lois. "We were both raised on ranches north of Phoenix and had dreamed of having a place in the high country." After inquiring around the area, they found out that the ranch, originally destined to become a subdivision consisting of one hundred homes, was now in limbo due to the fact that in 1980 the developer had declared bankruptcy and abandoned the property. After two years of negotiating with the local bank, Lois and Jerry became owners of the ranch and its 123 acres of land all surrounded by a national forest.

The property, homesteaded in the late 1800s as a sheep ranch, consisted of four historic structures. "Considering their age, they were in remarkable condition," says Jerry. "There was no question that we

LEFT: One of the focal points of the new ranch house is a 4-ft.-wide, 25-ft.-high alligator bark juniper tree. After the tree was stripped of its leaves and treated with an insecticide, it was coated with a clear wood sealant. Once it was set in place, builder David Farr built the room around it.

RIGHT: The great room features both a majestic juniper tree and a 25-ft.-high stone fireplace. A woodstove, though not as stately as the fireplace, is the main source of heat in the room.

would restore the buildings and eventually make the old ranch house our home."

After spending a year cleaning up the property, they began working on restoring the original homestead cabin, which later became the ranch bunkhouse. The cabin, built in 1897, had walls of hand-hewn ponderosa pine timbers originally cut from the property. Restoration was done by Steve Larson, a local builder, and Jim Price, who lived on the property as a caretaker. Price, a master craftsman, did the majority of the work.

ABOVE: An eclectic collection of Native American arts and crafts lends an Old West spirit to the dining room. All of the light fixtures in the house were handmade by Jerry Jacka.

RIGHT: In the main house, the great room opens into a large state-of-the-art kitchen and dining area, complete with an island and peninsula. Flooring of poured concrete and slate tile is used throughout to connect the different areas of the house.

OPPOSITE: The large antique Spanish-style sideboard displays a mix of old and new pottery. Metal spiral stairs lead up to Lois Jacka's office in the loft area.

Because there was no electric service to this remote location, the couple decided to use solar energy. An array of 48 solar panels, complete with batteries and a state-of-the-art power inverter, was installed to provide the adequate 120-volt electricity for the ranch. While the solar panels were being installed, Jerry and Lois proceeded to add 3,000 square feet to the historic ranch house's original 900 square feet. Their plan was to have the new section carefully designed to blend in with the original structure.

Lois Jacka's office is in the loft area, perched on top of the alligator bark juniper tree, giving her a bird's-eye view of the great room below.

Next came the restoration of the original ranch house built between 1910 and 1912. Up to this point, the Jackas had been living part-time on the property while continuing to work on their photography and writing assignments. After ten years of commuting to the ranch, they decided to retire and devote all of their time to further improving their dream home.

Early into the project, the Jackas hired local builder David Farr to work on the addition with his sons Jefer and Daven. The Farrs heard about a huge sawmill owned by the Navajo Nation that had recently closed. Located north of Window Rock, Arizona, the mill, built in the early 1950s, was being dismantled and the materials sold. This was good news to Jerry and Lois because several of the huge timbers that formed the floor in one of the buildings closely matched the hand-hewn timbers of the old ranch house. They decided to purchase these timbers, along with hundreds of feet of antique tongue-and-groove pine lumber plus sheets of oxidized tin, to be included in the new addition to the house.

The Farrs used the reclaimed wood throughout the building, carefully hand-crafting dovetail joint corners to match the ones in the original structure. Oxidized tin used for the roofing on the old and new structures also created a visual connection.

One of the focal points of the new ranch house is a 4-foot wide, 25-foot high alligator bark juniper tree that was placed in the middle of the great room. After getting a permit from the U.S. Forest Service, Jerry and Lois had David Farr cut and haul the tree three miles to the building site.

The Jackas were able to preserve the old buildings and create a comfortable retirement retreat for themselves, all the while maintaining the natural beauty of the land. Rescued from the developer's wrecking ball, this once rundown ranch has been given a new lease on life as both a beloved new home and an example of the importance of historic restoration.

OPPOSITE: In the master bedroom, the interior walls are covered in a light-pine paneling that provides an attractive contrast to the rough-cut timbers of the outside walls. The house also has two guest bedrooms, an office, three baths, and a loft.

ABOVE: The master bath features hand-crafted vanity countertops of resin-coated alligator juniper. An oval whirlpool tub is set into a juniper-wood platform with a travertine-tile backsplash.

RIGHT: Early ranch owners brought furnishings from Mexico to dress up their rustic homes. This elegant antique side-board is representative of the style that was popular among nineteenth-century ranchers.

"Many of the building materials were salvaged from a recently closed historic sawmill built by the Navajo Nation."

A Lakeside Retreat

Designed as an informal getaway, this log home features year-round seasonal views.

OPPOSITE: Tucked into the woods, this log-home retreat is a mix of modern and rustic architecture designed to take advantage of the stunning view of the lake.

ABOVE: The great room has a cathedral ceiling with knotty pine tongue-and-groove paneling, log beams, and two collar ties running the length of the room, which allows for a more open floor plan.

There is something inherently beautiful about the combination of lakefront property and a log home—they just naturally go together. Such is the case for this year-round 2,450-square-foot retreat located on a lake in Lac du Flambeau, Wisconsin.

An ideal design for its natural surroundings, this "Prow Style" home, built by Tomahawk Log & Country Homes in Tomahawk, Wisconsin, features an entire wall of floor-to-ceiling windows and doors that overlook the lakefront. This expansive wall of glass has a slightly angled prow front that creates a visual rhythm to invite you inside, while at the same time opening the great room to magnificent year-round seasonal views of the lake and forests.

Working in close collaboration with salesman/designer Troy Gullo, the homeowners chose an existing Tomahawk floor plan called the "Willow Glen," then made

Attention to detail is evident in the geometric pattern of the stairway leading to the loft. The fieldstone fireplace with a custom log mantel provides a dramatic and cozy touch but little heat. Instead, a forced-air system is used to heat the entire house.

"The house seems to be built with full-round logs, but it's actually made of 12-inch half-log construction."

alterations to fit their own personal needs.

Designed as a gathering place for friends and family, the layout features a kitchen and dining room that open to the great room for easy entertaining.

The focal point of the great room is its natural fieldstone fireplace, reaching up 23 feet to the height of the cathedral ceiling. A private master-bedroom suite is located in the loft area away from the public rooms. Two more bedrooms are situated on the main floor, as well as a full bath.

The design of the house also allowed for a future renovation of the living space. While planning the mechanical systems, such as plumbing and heating, the layout was devised to allow for expansion. This wise planning came to fruition recently when the family decided to convert the basement area into a family room complete with a gas stove, kitchenette, and laundry room.

The exterior of the house has a large covered porch on the west side and a magnificent deck that covers the south side

LEFT: Off to one side of the great room, overlooking the deck with its views of the lake, the dining area is the essence of simplicity. A traditional chandelier adds an elegant touch to the room.

ABOVE: The family dog, Sylvie, relaxes on the side porch. Located on the west side of the house, the porch was built to take advantage of the water views.

OPPOSITE: Knotty-pine cabinets, joined with light-green solid-surfacing countertops, seamlessly flow into the cabin's great room. Above the granite-top island, three mica pendant task lights impart a craftsman-style ambiance to the room.

RIGHT: High ceilings and traditional-style arched windows turn the loft area's master bedroom into a spacious, light-filled retreat. Smooth knotty-pine paneling balances with the rustic log walls.

OPPOSITE TOP: Situated on the main floor, this cozy guest room has an Adirondack-style log bed featuring a cutout woodland motif on the headboard. Above the headboard are old cabin-style prints.

OPPOSITE BOTTOM: This child's room was designed with plenty of space for sleepovers. The light-green bunk beds provide a nice contrast to the room's abundance of wood.

of the house overlooking the lake. Constructed of treated pine, the deck design follows the line of the prow shape, completely integrating it with the house. The outside of the house seems to be built with full-round logs. Actually, it is made of 12-inch northern white pine half-log construction on the outside and a combination of 8-inch round half-logs, and classic lakeside knotty-pine paneling on the inside. With Tomahawk's "Energy Log System," using half logs not only enables the fabrication of larger windows and a more flexible floor plan than a full-log building, it also allows for insertion of standard insulation between the walls—creating an energy-saving feature.

The homeowners continued this eco-friendly construction by using reclaimed wood for all of the floors throughout the house. The flooring materials were salvaged from old buildings then resawn, replaned, and refinished. The result is a beautiful, warm wood product with a time-weathered look that is coveted by many log-home owners.

A Classic Cabin

This rustic Michigan retreat is a natural beauty.

While residing in their traditional frame house in northern Michigan, Sally and Jay Olson decided to redecorate their family room in a rustic cabin theme. This was only the beginning of their fascination with log-home living.

In 2003 after several years of planning, they moved into a new custom-made log home. The house is located near Harvard Spring, Michigan, off Highway M 119—a verdant area referred to by the locals as the "Highway of Trees." It sits on a bluff overlooking Five-Mile Creek—one of several bodies of water that feed into northern Lake Michigan. The structure is made of red pine, a wood native to Michigan. "We wanted to use as many local materials as possible," says Sally. "The design of the log home is so natural that we felt it would be logical to use indigenous products."

The project began to take hold when the Olsons contacted Maple Island Log Homes in Twin Lake, Michigan. "We supplied the log package for the project," says Eric Gordon, vice president of Maple Island. "The house was first erected at our log yard in Michigan, then disassembled and taken to the homeowner's site where it

LEFT: Enabling family and guests to drive up to the entrance of the house, a large portico-like structure is framed by 12-in. logs and provides shelter from inclement weather.

RIGHT: The house is a hand-crafted log structure with saddle-notched corners and full-log gables that call to mind Asian architecture. Overlooking a creek, the architecture includes both open and covered deck areas for sun or shade.

LEFT, TOP: Situated right off the kitchen area and surrounded by windows, this comfortable dining nook, featuring a hand-cast tile floor with radiant heat, is decorated in the style of a 1940s lakeside cabin.

LEFT, BOTTOM: A bright burst of yellow wall frames the entry into the kitchen. Although large, the kitchen retains a cottage feel, thanks to the painted checkered floor pattern and knotty-pine cabinets. The large, red, granite-top island adds to the rich color scheme.

OPPOSITE: The focal point of the living room is the cultured-stone fireplace and a cozy sitting area. Upholstered in soft distressed red leather, the seating provides a textural contrast to the room's abundance of wood and stone.

was re-erected." The company only makes handcrafted log homes. Each full log is hand-peeled using a drawknife, an age-old method that brings out the beauty and grain of the wood. Every log is individually scribed, notched, and fitted into position. This method requires skill to ensure that the notching of each log is not only inherently tight, but visibly tight. The result is a log that looks more natural than a machine-milled log.

Working with on-staff architects and designers, the Olsons poured over plans, revisited pages from magazines, and gathered ideas to create a distinctive house that looks and functions the way they wanted.

The personal details that were put into the home are evident throughout its rooms and especially in the great room. The space features a soaring 25-foot cathedral ceiling with a towering fireplace surrounded by walls of solid logs. The fireplace is constructed of cultured stone, a veneer material made of lightweight aggregate that is one-quarter the weight of stone. Because of the height of the fireplace, actual stones would be too heavy. Each piece of cultured stone was carefully chosen to replicate native stones found in and around

Dramatic log-framed windows bring the outdoors inside to the two-story great room. Jay's baby grand piano is a perfect fit in the large, open room.

Michigan. The exterior also features the same cultured stone in the stacked rock foundations. The placement of the stone not only adds to the natural landscaping, it also protects the logs from water splashes. All of the decks are constructed of white cedar, a decay and insect-resistant wood that weathers to a pleasing light gray. The roofing is a fiberglass shingle that is treated with a mold-resistant finish.

Measuring 3,200 square feet, the main house consists of three floors, including a lower level, plus a loft area. The large great room's windows extend into the second level of the house, flooding the room with natural light. Upstairs there is an open loft with a guest room, office, game room, and full bath with open views of Lake Michigan. The main floor has the great room, kitchen, formal dining room, and breakfast nook. Designed with plenty of entertainment amenities, the lower level has a TV room and a sitting room with a gas fireplace.

Although the house is new, it is designed in the spirit of country log cabins that were so popular in the 1940s and 50s. The result is a log home that is both impressive and inviting.

"Each log is hand-peeled using a drawknife, an age-old method that brings out the beauty and grain of the wood."

Into the Woods

A down-home, southern-style cabin is the perfect mix of old and new.

After years of traveling each weekend from her city job in Atlanta, Georgia, to her small cabin retreat in the north Georgia mountains, Betty Hemrick decided to give up urban living for a more relaxing rural lifestyle. Opting for a new log home, she purchased land in Blue Ridge, Georgia, not far from her weekend cabin.

Working with Cheryle Dupont of Sisson Dupont & Carder Premium Logs and Timber Products, (also in Blue Ridge), Hemrick chose a 1,626-square-foot, mountain-style cabin from the company's standard floor plans, adjusting it to fit her personal needs.

The cabin is constructed of 6 x 12-inch full logs of eastern white pine with dovetail corners, a chink groove, and hand-hewn finish. On-staff designers working closely with Hemrick created a cozy yet spacious home that includes two levels, a loft, great room, dining room, two bedrooms, and two baths. All of the floors throughout the house are wide-plank ponderosa pine with a fruitwood stain.

The house sits on one acre of land

ABOVE: Overlooking a view of the mountains, the cabin's wide screened-in porch also functions as an outdoor room complete with a classic porch swing. The overhead fan provides a cool breeze for hot summer nights.

OPPOSITE: All of the outdoor flooring is pressure-treated pine. The open-porch setting is not only a nice place to sit and chat, it also serves as an entrance—the perfect place to welcome visitors.

ABOVE: Pine cabinets with a fruitwood finish and chocolate glaze visually connect the galley kitchen with the rest of the house. Stainless-steel appliances, granite counters, and stainless-steel sinks provide a sleek and welcome contrast to the wood surfaces.

LEFT: The geometric-pattern cornices in the great room were designed by Betty and built by a local craftsman out of pine board, birch bark, and hickory branches.

RIGHT: The antique hickory dining table and chairs, one of a pair of realistic-looking resin antler chandeliers, an old TV cabinet trimmed with hickory branches, and birch-bark cornices create the essence of an Adirondack-style log cabin.

surrounded by open fields and mountain views. Outside living areas include a screened-in porch and a covered entryway large enough for a small table and chairs. Although the house is considered small, the abundance of windows and high ceilings make it appear larger than it is. The focal point in the great room is a wood-burning fireplace made of Arkansas fieldstone that rises to the ceiling height of 22 feet.

Hemrick, who once studied interior design and now works for Sisson Dupont & Carder, furnished the house with items from both her home in Atlanta as well as her previous weekend cabin. She filled the house with a mix of antiques and hand-made items. "I kept an eye on my budget,

taking care not to go overboard," she admits. "Fortunately my daughter, who is a very talented craftsperson, provided a lot of the accessories—including beautiful hand-made pottery pieces and birch-bark lamps. She and I also made several of the hand-woven baskets that are displayed through-out the house."

With an eye for a bargain and her love of antiques, Henrick was able to fill the house with a mix of comfortable eclectic furnishings that suit the scale of the cabin's rooms. "I wanted to create a natural, laid-back look so that visitors would always feel relaxed," she says. The result is a home that has a warm, lived-in look without being over decorated.

BELOW: Betty filled the master bedroom with a collection of found objects and antiques. Her eye for unique design is evident in her creation of a rhododendron-bark curtain rod over the window.

OPPOSITE, TOP LEFT: With a magnificent view of the mountains, the loft area is a perfect place to hang out and relax. Furnished with a sleep sofa and twin beds, it also doubles as the grand-children's room when they come to visit.

OPPOSITE, TOP RIGHT: This catwalk leading to the loft area overlooks the great room below. A catwalk is a popular architectural feature in log homes because it creates a feeling of interior spaciousness.

OPPOSITE, BOTTOM: Designed as a restful retreat, the country-style master bath features a contemporary whirlpool tub set in a platform that provides a convenient hiding place for routing pipes. The mirror over the sink was fashioned from an old picture frame.

Constructed of 6x12-inch full logs of eastern white pine, the cabin was designed with dovetail corners, a chink groove, and hand-hewn finish. The roof is covered in architectural shingles set in a random pattern that creates a rustic look.

Ski Country

The ultimate Catskill Mountain vacation home

In 2000, Julie and Mario Galdi—who live in New Jersey—decided to merge their love of skiing and log homes and started looking for the perfect place for their vacation getaway. After spending many years traveling around the United States on ski vacations, the Galdis decided on Windham, New York, as the ideal place for their log home.

This mountainous area of upstate New York is a popular resort area, especially for skiers. What better place to build their home than here, which is near Catskill Park, a protected forest preserve with a view of the Catskill Mountain range.

They had always wanted a log home. "Whenever we skied out west, we always admired the rustic architecture of the lodges where we stayed. We fell in love with the log style," says Julie. "Over the years, I had also started a collection of log-home magazines, which came in handy once we started the actual planning."

Once the Galdis were ready to build, they put together a team of professionals to help them make it happen. Mario, a mechanical contractor by trade, called Jim Diana of LAN Associates in Goshen, New

LEFT: The front of the house features a classical-style triangular pediment in a full facade, with stripped log columns resting on fieldstone bases. A large deck includes a gazebo and hot tub to warm up the winter days.

RIGHT: This 3,437-sq.-ft. house is made up of half-log construction with a conventional frame of 2x6 stud walls complete with insulation, sheathing, and a vapor barrier.

180

The Galdis decided to make the loft area a game room complete with a full-size pool table. In keeping with the country setting, the couple had their portrait painted in a Grant Wood American-Gothic style.

York—a talented architect he knew through industry contacts. Diana worked very closely with the family for over a year designing the 3,437-square-foot house, making sure that the site would take advantage of the location's incredible views of the nearby mountain range. After researching their options, the Galdis chose Expedition Log Homes in Oostburg, Wisconsin, to provide the logs, prepare the blueprints, and make any small modifications that the Galdis needed.

Made up of half-log construction, the house is built with conventional 2x6 stud walls. The Galdis selected cedar for the exterior walls and a mix of pine and cedar for the interior walls of the house. The rooms of the house are not all finished alike. Some feature flat- or round-log walls. Others have been finished with wallboard or knotty-pine paneling.

The house is large, with its great room, kitchen, dining room, and five bedrooms as a well as a loft space, and three and a half bathrooms. The finished basement is complete with a guest room, another bathroom, laundry room, and storage space. The walk-out basement, used by friends and family when departing for or returning from the slopes, is a convenient place for putting on or taking off ski gear.

Personal attention was given to each of the rooms, especially the great room where a 30-foot-high, cultured-stone fireplace serves not only as the focal point but as the favorite place to gather après ski. The impressive fireplace structure is balanced by the room's floor-to-ceiling windows that span the entire front of the building, opening the great room to the spectacular view outside.

The fireplace isn't the only source of heat in the house. For more efficient heating, there is also a wood-burning stove and radiant in-floor heating that Mario himself

LEFT: The great room's soaring window wall provides spectacular views of the nearby mountain range while filling the room with natural light. The tie beams and king posts are structural beams; the log rafters are simply decorative.

BELOW: Because they love to cook and entertain, the Galdis paid close attention to the layout of the kitchen. Besides installing the state-of-the-art appliances, they made sure the cabinets had enough storage for their needs.

OPPOSITE: Because of the 30-ft. height of the fireplace, cultured stone—a manufactured stone veneer made of light-weight aggregate material that is approximatly one-quarter the weight of full-thickness stone—was used.

OPPOSITE: Stepping away from the rustic-cabin look, the master bath has patterned walls, mission-style cabinets, slate flooring, and a state-of-the-art walk-in shower tiled in slate.

RIGHT: Located off of the loft area, this light-filled guest room, painted in a rich cranberry, offers soft wall-to-wall carpeting and a private balcony.

BELOW: The master bedroom was designed so the couple have views of the mountains through the French doors and from their deck. The log bed harmonizes beautifully with the hand-hewn beams and log walls.

installed in each of the rooms. Clean, quiet, and energy efficient, radiant heating can be separated into zones, or in this case rooms. This selective heating offers flexibility for a vacation home because the house is not always filled with guests.

The exterior of the house is designed for outdoor living. It's elevated balconies and open gable porch, as well as the wraparound deck, provide space for alfresco dining, lounging, and panoramic views of both Windham and Hunter Mountain.

Aside from the convenience of being so close to the ski slopes in the winter, an added bonus of the Galdis' home is the delightful display of colors and textures that nature provides as its setting year-round.

Planning Ahead

A lakeside home designed for future retirement living

The Northwoods section of Phelps, Wisconsin, is known for its beautiful acres of forests, lakes, and clean air. It is a natural location for retirement living for many people who find it ideal for empty-nesters. Choosing a location that will provide all of the activities and amenities desired for a comfortable lifestyle is key for these homeowners.

Although Frank and Kathy Arnold aren't ready to retire just yet, they did want to plan ahead, and Phelps seemed like the perfect place to them, too. Their dream log home could segue from a weekend house to a suitable, comfort-filled retirement retreat.

This wasn't the family's first log cabin. Frank, a veterinarian, in Hinsdale, Illinois, owned a small log cabin next door to his office. "Kathy and I really liked the natural look of the cabin. It inspired us to build a full-size log home," he says.

Once the Arnolds found their five acres of property on a lake in Phelps, they contacted Tomahawk Log & Country Homes in Tomahawk, Wisconsin, to help them get

LEFT: The expansive great room, a mix of glass, stone, and wood, features a large prow-shaped wall of windows and doors. Natural harmonious colors run through the Michigan fieldstone that covers the fireplace wall.

RIGHT: An open deck runs the length of the lakeside. At one end of the deck, this covered porch serves as a place to store wet gear after a day of fishing or to hang out on a rainy day.

Lofts are a great way to expand space without closing in a room. The Arnolds turned their loft into a guest room. The daybed doubles as seating and the chest is used as a table and storage unit.

started. The couple decided on a "Prow Style" home with a deck that runs the length of the lakeside of the house. The design also includes an entire wall of floor-to-ceiling windows and doors that overlook the lakefront. Watching the change of seasons from the expansive wall of glass is one of the bonuses the Arnolds really love about the view.

The home was designed from one of Tomahawk's existing plans and then modified by the homeowners with the help of salesman/designer Troy Gullo.

The construction was done by Dan Benson Builders of Land O' Lakes, Wisconsin. The house is 2,779 square feet and made of 12-inch northern white pine half-log construction on the outside and a combination of 8-inch round half logs and knotty-pine

LEFT: This eat-in kitchen with its wood cathedral ceiling promotes a sense of spaciousness and inviting comfort. Cove lighting installed in the architectural cornice frames the room while highlighting the warm knotty-pine walls and cabinets.

BELOW: A large fieldstone wood-burning fireplace creates a relaxed, yet rustic ambiance in the master bedroom. A pair of French doors leads to the deck, which has views of the lake.

OPPOSITE: The entrance was designed with a pitched-roof portico that provides cover for family and visitors. Michigan fieldstone is used in the stacked-rock foundations—a great protection against water splash-up damage to the logs.

paneling on the inside. By using Tomahawk's half-log "Energy Log System," Benson Builders were able to fabricate larger windows and a more flexible floor plan than if they were using full logs. The half-log system also allows for insertion of standard insulation between the walls—a popular and energy-saving feature.

Keeping in mind that it would be designed as the Arnold's future retirement home as well as their current weekend retreat, the floor plan is basically one level except for a loft guest room. Choosing a single-level design for a retirement home is a wise choice because of its easy access and maintenance. A loft, on the other hand, offers extra sleeping space. Climbing up to the loft may not be something older folks want to do on a regular basis, but most

> "The great room design also includes an entire wall of floor-to-ceiling windows and doors that overlook the lakefront."

younger guests will not have a problem with the stairs. The Arnolds' layout also includes a great room that overlooks the lake, an eat-in kitchen, master bedroom, two full bathrooms, a home office, and a mudroom.

The focal point of the great room is its Michigan fieldstone-fireplace wall that reaches up 23 feet to the top of the cathedral ceiling. The ceiling is knotty-pine paneling with two large log collar ties running the length of the room. The combination of stone and logs continues from the interior to the exterior for a harmonious blend. The Arnolds chose an area near a lake—but not too close to cause flooding problems. It's the perfect location for outdoor activities including canoeing, fishing, and swimming, or simply relaxing with friends.

8

Log-Home Plans

 hinking of building your own dream log home? The following pages feature log-home plans that you can purchase. Selecting a predesigned log home can save you thousands of dollars in comparison to the cost of one that is custom designed. However, all of these predesigned plans, which have been created by a variety of top home designers from all over the country, can be customized to meet your individual tastes and needs.

Decide What Type of Plan Package You Need

How many Plans Should You Order?

Standard 8-Set Package. We've found that our 8-set package is the best value for someone who is ready to start building. The 8-set package provides plans for you, your builder, the subcontractors, mortgage lender, and the building department.

Minimum 5-Set Package. If you are in the bidding process, you may want to order only five sets for the bidding round and reorder additional sets as needed.

1-Set Study Package. The 1-set package allows you to review your home plan in detail. The plan will be marked as a study print, and it is illegal to build a house from a study print alone. It is a violation of copyright law to reproduce a blueprint without permission.

Buying Additional Sets

If you require additional copies of blueprints for your home construction, you can order additional sets within 60 days of the original order date at a reduced price. The cost is $45.00 for each additional set. For more information, contact customer service.

Reproducible Masters

If you plan to make minor changes to one of our home plans, you can purchase reproducible masters. These plans are printed on bond or vellum paper that is easy to alter. They clearly indicate your right to modify, copy, or reproduce the plans. Reproducible masters allow an architect, designer, or builder to alter our plans to give you a customized home design. This package also allows you to print as many copies of the modified plans as you need for the construction of one home.

CAD (Computer Aided Design) Files

CAD files are the complete set of home plans in an electronic file format. Choose this option if there are multiple changes you wish made to the home plans and you have a local design professional able to make the changes. Not available for all plans. Please contact our order department or visit our Web site to check the availability of CAD files for your plan.

Mirror-Reverse Sets/Right-Reading Reverse

Plans can be printed in mirror-reverse—we can "flip" plans to create a mirror image of the design. This is useful when the house would fit your site or personal preferences if all the rooms were on the opposite side than shown. As the image is reversed, the lettering and dimensions will also be reversed, meaning they will read backwards. Therefore, when ordering mirror-reverse drawings, you must order at least one set of the original plan unreversed. A $50.00 fee per plan order will be charged for mirror-reverse (regardless of the number of mirror-reverse sets ordered). Some plans are available in right-reading reverse, this feature will show the plan in reverse, but the writing on the plan will be readable. A $150.00 fee per plan order will be charged for right-reading reverse (regardless of the number of right-reading reverse sets ordered). Please contact our order department or visit our website to check the availibility of this feature for your chosen plan.

EZ Quote: Home Cost Estimator

EZ Quote is our response to one of the most frequently asked questions we hear from customers: "How much will the house cost me to build?" EZ Quote: Home Cost Estimator will enable you to obtain a calculated building cost to construct your home, based on labor rates and building material costs within your zip code area. This summary is useful for those who want to get an idea of the total construction costs before purchasing sets of home plans. It will also provide a level of comfort when you begin soliciting bids. The cost is $29.95 for the first EZ Quote and $19.95 for each additional one. Available only in the U.S. and Canada.

Materials List

Available for most of our plans, the Materials List provides you an invaluable resource in planning and estimating the cost of your home. Each Materials List outlines the quantity, dimensions, and type of materials needed to build your home (with the exception of mechanical systems). You will get faster, more-accurate bids from your contractors and building suppliers. A Materials List may only be ordered with the purchase of at least five sets of home plans.

CompleteCost Estimator

CompleteCost Estimator is a valuable tool for use in planning and constructing your new home. It provides more detail than a materials list and will act as a checklist for all items you will need to select or coordinate during your building process. CompleteCost Estimator is only available for certain plans (please see Plan Index) and may only be ordered with the purchase of at least five sets of home plans. The cost is $125.00 for CompleteCost Estimator.

Order Toll Free by Phone
1-800-523-6789
By Fax: 201-760-2431

Orders received 3PM ET, will be processed and shipped within two business days.

Order Online
www.ultimateplans.com

Mail Your Order
Creative Homeowner
Attn: Home Plans
24 Park Way
Upper Saddle River, NJ 07458

Canadian Customers
Order Toll Free 1-800-393-1883

Mail Your Order (Canada)
Creative Homeowner Canada
Attn: Home Plans
113-437 Martin St., Ste. 215
Penticton, BC V2A 5L1

Before You Order

Our Exchange Policy

Blueprints are nonrefundable. However, should you find that the plan you have purchased does not fit your needs, you may exchange that plan for another plan in our collection within 60 days from the date of your original order. The entire content of your original order must be returned before an exchange will be processed. You will be charged a processing fee of 20% of the amount of the original order, the cost difference between the new plan set and the original plan set (if applicable), and all related shipping costs for the new plans. Contact our order department for more information. Please note: reproducible masters may only be exchanged if the package is unopened and CAD files cannot be exchanged and are nonrefundable.

Building Codes and Requirements

All plans offered for sale in this book and on our website (www.ultimateplans.com) are continually updated to meet the latest International Residential Code (IRC). Because building codes vary from area to area, some drawing modifications and/or the assistance of a professional designer or architect may be necessary to comply with your local codes or to accommodate specific building site conditions. We strongly advise you to consult with your local building official for information regarding codes governing your area.

Multiple Plan Discount

Purchase **3** different home plans in the **same order** and receive **5% off** the plan price.

Purchase **5** or more different home plans in the **same order** and receive **10% off** the plan price.

(Please Note: Study sets do not apply.)

Blueprint Price Schedule

Price Code	1 Set	5 Sets	8 Sets	Reproducible Masters	CAD	Materials List
A	$400	$440	$475	$575	$1,025	$85
B	$440	$525	$555	$685	$1,195	$85
C	$510	$575	$635	$740	$1,265	$85
D	$560	$605	$665	$800	$1,300	$95
E	$600	$675	$705	$845	$1,400	$95
F	$650	$725	$775	$890	$1,500	$95
G	$720	$790	$840	$950	$1,600	$95
H	$820	$860	$945	$1,095	$1,700	$95
I	$945	$975	$1,075	$1,195	$1,890	$105
J	$1,010	$1,080	$1,125	$1,250	$1,900	$105
K	$1,125	$1,210	$1,250	$1,380	$2,030	$105
L	$1,240	$1,335	$1,375	$1,535	$2,270	$105

Note: All prices subject to change

Shipping & Handling

	1-4 Sets	5-7 Sets	8+ Sets or Reproducibles	CAD
US Regular (7–10 business days)	$18	$20	$25	$25
US Priority (3–5 business days)	$25	$30	$35	$35
US Express (1–2 business days)	$40	$45	$50	$50
Canada Express (1–2 business days)	$100	$100	$100	$100
Worldwide Express (3–5 business days)	Quote Required			

Note: All delivery times are from date the blueprint package is shipped (typically within 1-2 days of placing order).

Order Form   Please send me the following:

Plan Number: _____ **Price Code:** _____ (See Plan Index.)

Indicate Foundation Type: (Select ONE. See plan page for availability.)

❏ Slab   ❏ Crawl space   ❏ Basement   ❏ Walk-out basement

❏ Optional Foundation for Fee _____ $_____
(Please enter foundation here)

*Please call all our order department or visit our website for optional foundation fee

Basic Blueprint Package   Cost

❏ CAD Files $_____
❏ Reproducible Masters $_____
❏ 8-Set Plan Package $_____
❏ 5-Set Plan Package $_____
❏ 1-Set Study Package $_____
❏ Additional plan sets:
    __ sets at $45.00 per set $_____
❏ Print in mirror-reverse: $50.00 per order $_____
    *Please call all our order department or visit our website for availibility
❏ Print in right-reading reverse: $150.00 per order $_____
    *Please call all our order department or visit our website for availibility

Important Extras

❏ Materials List $_____
❏ CompleteCost Materials Report at $125.00 $_____
    Zip Code of Home/Building Site _____
❏ EZ Quote for Plan #_____ at $29.95 $_____
❏ Additional EZ Quotes for Plan #s_____ $_____
    at $19.95 each
Shipping (see chart above) $_____
SUBTOTAL $_____
Sales Tax (NJ residents only, add 7%) $_____
TOTAL $_____

Order Toll Free: 1-800-523-6789   By Fax: 201-760-2431
Creative Homeowner (Home Plans Order Dept.)
24 Park Way
Upper Saddle River, NJ 07458

Name _____
               (Please print or type)

Street _____
               (Please do not use a P.O. Box)

City _____ State _____

Country _____ Zip _____

Daytime telephone ( ) _____

Fax ( ) _____
               (Required for reproducible orders)

E-Mail _____

Payment ❏ Bank check/money order. No personal checks.
               Make checks payable to Creative Homeowner

❏ VISA   ❏ MasterCard   ❏ American Express   ❏ Discover

Credit card number _____

Expiration date (mm/yy) _____

Signature _____

Please check the appropriate box:
❏ Building home for myself   ❏ Building home for someone else

SOURCE CODE | CA607

197

Plan #451015

Dimensions: 67' W x 67'6" D
Levels: 2
Square Footage: 2,113
Main Level Sq. Ft.: 1,898
Upper Level Sq. Ft.: 215
Bedrooms: 3
Bathrooms: 2
Foundation: Crawl space
Material List Available: No
Price Category: D

Images provided by designer/architect.

This wonderful home is perfect for you and your family.

Features:

• **Great Room:** This large two-story great room is a wonderful place for family and friends to gather and relax.
• **Master Suite:** You'll love being in this master suite, with its large bedroom area, walk-in closet, and bathroom with dual sinks.

• **Secondary Bedrooms:** Two additional bedrooms are located on the opposite side of the home from the master suite.
• **Garage:** The location of this two-car garage to the house creates a driveway area that the children can play in while easily being watched from the home. In addition, the garage is conveniently in close proximity to the kitchen, making trips with groceries even easier.

CAD FILE AVAILABLE

Main Level Floor Plan

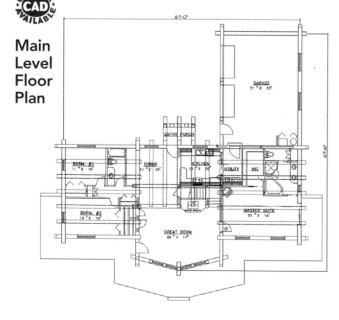

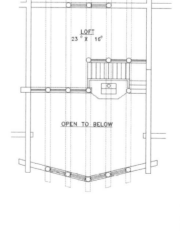

Upper Level Floor Plan

Copyright by designer/architect.

Rear View

Plan #451002

Dimensions: 56' W x 44' D
Levels: 2
Square Footage: 3,303
Main Level Sq. Ft.: 1,901
Upper Level Sq. Ft.: 1,402
Bedrooms: 3
Bathrooms: 2
Foundation: Crawl space or basement
Material List Available: No
Price Category: G

Images provided by designer/architect.

A beautiful deck area perfect for entertaining or relaxing with friends and family accentuates this home.

Features:

- Decks: Multiple deck areas throughout the first and second stories of the home make enjoying the outdoors easy and fun for you and your guests.
- Living Room: This stunning two-story living room is perfect for parties or quiet evenings, whichever suits your needs.
- Kitchen: Function meets style in this conveniently located kitchen. A center island workspace helps to get all of your meals to the table with less stress.
- Master Suite: Up the spiral staircase is a spacious master suite, featuring a walk-in closet, and two vanity areas.

Main Level Floor Plan

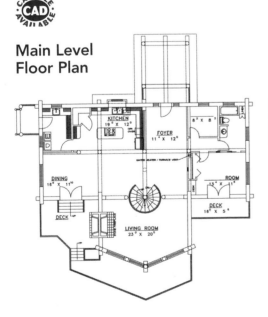

Upper Level Floor Plan

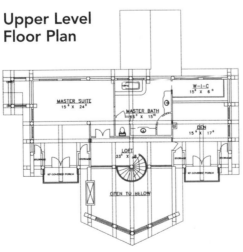

Lower Level Floor Plan

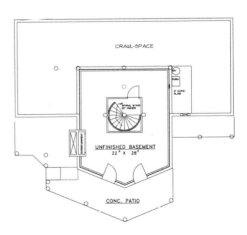

Copyright by designer/architect.

Plan #451003

Dimensions: 48'10" W x 57' D

Levels: 2

Square Footage: 2,263

Main Level Sq. Ft.: 1,412

Upper Level Sq. Ft.: 851

Bedrooms: 2

Bathrooms: 2

Foundation: Slab

Material List Available: No

Price Category: E

Images provided by designer/architect.

CAD FILE AVAILABLE

Main Level Floor Plan

Upper Level Floor Plan

Lower Level Floor Plan

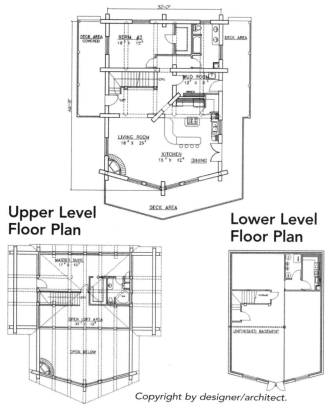

Copyright by designer/architect.

Plan #151801

Dimensions: 45'8" W x 41'8" D

Levels: 1.5

Square Footage: 1,658

Main Level Sq. Ft.: 1,002

Upper Level Sq. Ft.: 656

Bedrooms: 3

Bathrooms: 2

Foundation: Crawl space

CompleteCost List Available: Yes

Price Category: C

Images provided by designer/architect.

Main Level Floor Plan

Upper Level Floor Plan

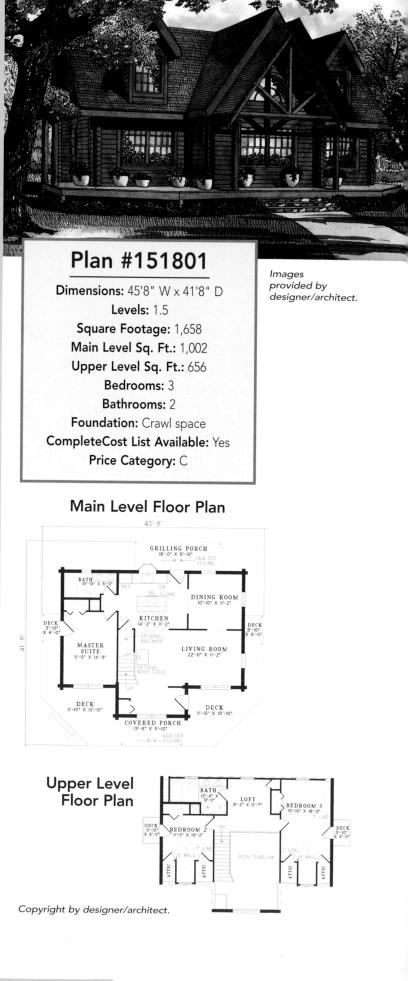

Copyright by designer/architect.

200

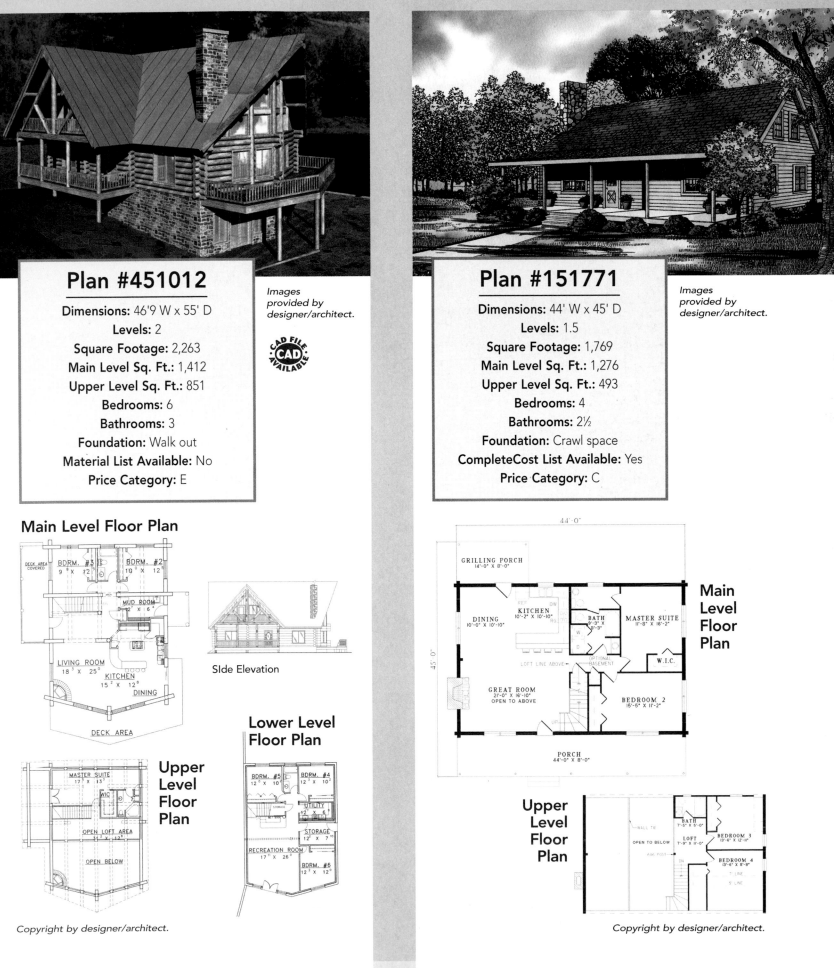

Plan #451012

Dimensions: 46'9 W x 55' D

Levels: 2

Square Footage: 2,263

Main Level Sq. Ft.: 1,412

Upper Level Sq. Ft.: 851

Bedrooms: 6

Bathrooms: 3

Foundation: Walk out

Material List Available: No

Price Category: E

Images provided by designer/architect.

CAD FILE CAD AVAILABLE

Main Level Floor Plan

DECK AREA COVERED

BDRM. #3
9'8 X 12'5

BDRM. #2
10'0 X 12'5

MUD ROOM
9'2 X 6'5

LIVING ROOM
18'3 X 25'0

KITCHEN
15'2 X 12'8

DINING

DECK AREA

Side Elevation

Upper Level Floor Plan

MASTER SUITE
17'7 X 13'3

WIC

OPEN LOFT AREA
11'2 X 12'8

OPEN BELOW

Lower Level Floor Plan

BDRM. #5
12'2 X 10'4

BDRM. #4
12'3 X 10'2

STORAGE

UTILITY
12'2 X 6'9

STORAGE
12'2 X 7'0

RECREATION ROOM
17'11 X 26'0

BDRM. #6
12'2 X 12'0

Copyright by designer/architect.

Plan #151771

Dimensions: 44' W x 45' D

Levels: 1.5

Square Footage: 1,769

Main Level Sq. Ft.: 1,276

Upper Level Sq. Ft.: 493

Bedrooms: 4

Bathrooms: 2½

Foundation: Crawl space

CompleteCost List Available: Yes

Price Category: C

Images provided by designer/architect.

44'-0"

45'-0"

GRILLING PORCH
14'-0" X 8'-0"

DINING
10'-0" X 10'-10"

KITCHEN
10'-2" X 10'-10"

REF DW

RG

W D

BATH
9'-3" X

MASTER SUITE
11'-8" X 16'-2"

W.I.C.

LOFT LINE ABOVE

OPTIONAL BASEMENT

GREAT ROOM
21'-0" X 16'-10"
OPEN TO ABOVE

UP

BEDROOM 2
15'-5" X 11'-2"

PORCH
44'-0" X 8'-0"

Main Level Floor Plan

Upper Level Floor Plan

WALL TIE

OPEN TO BELOW

AXE POST

BATH
7'-5" X 5'-0"

LOFT
7'-9" X 11'-0"

BEDROOM 3
13'-6" X 12'-11"

BEDROOM 4
13'-6" X 8'-8"

DN

Copyright by designer/architect.

Plan #451062

Dimensions: 27' W x 30'8" D

Levels: 2

Square Footage: 1,485

Main Level Sq. Ft.: 972

Upper Level Sq. Ft.: 513

Bedrooms: 2

Bathrooms: 2

Foundation: Walk out

Material List Available: No

Price Category: B

This home makes the perfect vacation retreat.

Features:
- Kitchen/Dining Area: This space features plenty of counter area and room for multiple cooks in the kitchen.
- Living Room: Adjacent to the kitchen and dining area, this two-story living room is wonderful for entertaining guests or relaxing with your family.
- Master Suite: Upstairs, the master suite features two large closets, a tub, and a dual vanity.
- Garage: Downstairs, the two-car garage also features a shop area, perfect for working on a project or two.

Main Level Floor Plan

Upper Level Floor Plan

Lower Level Floor Plan

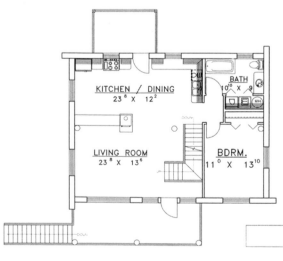

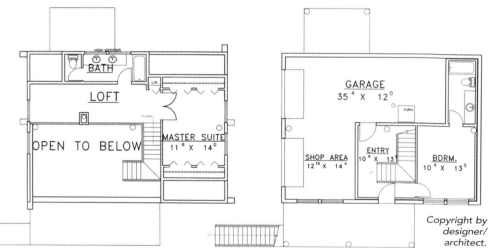

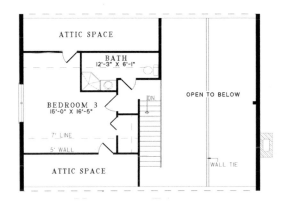

Plan #151747

Dimensions: 39' W x 36'10" D

Levels: 2

Square Footage: 1,477

Main Level Sq. Ft.: 1,131

Upper Level Sq. Ft.: 346

Bedrooms: 3

Bathrooms: 2

Foundation: Crawl space; basement or walk out for fee

CompleteCost List Available: Yes

Price Category: B

Images provided by designer/architect.

You'll step back into time when you come home to this simple log home with three bedrooms and a full covered porch.

Features:

• Great Room: This room with fireplace opens to the kitchen and dining area with a door to the rear yard.

• Kitchen: This U-shaped work area has an abundance of cabinets and counter space.

Enjoy the open feeling as you look into the great room.

• Master Bedroom: This main-level bedroom has two closets and a nearby bathroom and convenient laundry closet.

• Upper Level: The upper level has a bathroom with a corner shower and a large bedroom with attic-space access for seasonal storage.

Main Level Floor Plan

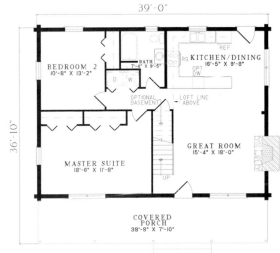

Upper Level Floor Plan

Copyright by designer/architect.

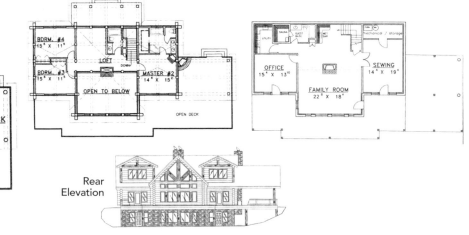

Plan #451035

Dimensions: 55' W x 44'4" D
Levels: 2
Square Footage: 2,883
Main Level Sq. Ft.: 1,622
Upper Level Sq. Ft.: 1,261
Bedrooms: 4
Bathrooms: 3½
Foundation: Walk out
Material List Available: No
Price Category: F

A large covered deck at the rear of this home is perfect for outdoor meals or spending time with friends and family.

Features:
- **Great Room:** This spacious great room surrounds an attractive fireplace, and opens out to the rear deck for outdoor entertaining.
- **Master Suites:** This home boasts two beautiful master suites, one upstairs and one downstairs, perfect for a guest suite or for an older child. They both feature a large bedroom area, dual sinks, and a walk-in closet.
- **Kitchen:** Surrounded by workspace, this kitchen is great for the home cook. A raised eating bar is a wonderful place for a quick snack or cup of coffee.

Main Level Floor Plan

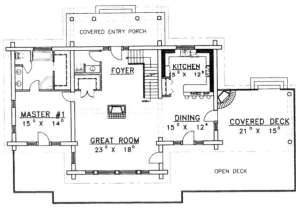

Upper Level Floor Plan

Lower Level Floor Plan

204

Plan #151751

Dimensions: 39'10" W x 39'8" D

Levels: 2

Square Footage: 1,449

Main Level Sq. Ft.: 1,059

Upper Level Sq. Ft.: 390

Bedrooms: 2

Bathrooms: 2½

Foundation: Crawl space; basement or walk out for fee

CompleteCost List Available: Yes

Price Category: B

Comfort is the key with this magnificent log home.

Features:

- Entry: Step up to the covered porch, which has two sets of French doors that open into the great room. Inside, you are greeted with a fireplace.
- Kitchen: Open to the great room, this cooking space has bar seating and view of a bay-shaped dining area.
- Master Suite: This main-level suite includes a large walk-in closet and a bath with an extra-large shower, double vanities, and a closet for a stacked washer and dryer.
- Upper Level: This space has a bedroom and bathroom with creative ceiling heights and a balcony view to the great room below.

Main Level Floor Plan

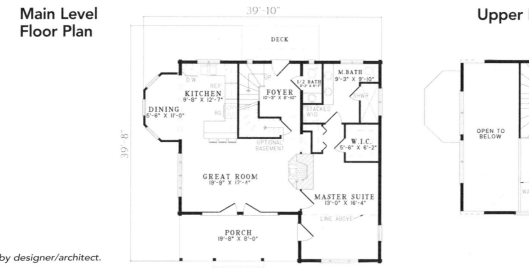

Upper Level Floor Plan

Plan #151752

Dimensions: 58' W x 40' D

Levels: 1.5

Square Footage: 2,402

Main Level Sq. Ft.: 1,584

Upper Level Sq. Ft.: 818

Bedrooms: 3

Bathrooms: 2½

Foundation: Crawl space; basement or walk out for fee

CompleteCost List Available: Yes

Price Category: E

Images provided by designer/architect.

Any mountain or picturesque building lot would be a terrific setting for this gorgeous log home.

Features:

• Great Room: Separating the master suite from the family areas that contain the kitchen and dining room, this central room provides each area with privacy.

• Dining Room: This room has French door access to the deck—perfect for grilling and after-dinner conversation.

• Master Suite: Complete with private bath and an entrance to the deck, this suite is located on the main level of the home.

• Kitchen: This large eat-in kitchen is open to the dining room and has a built-in pantry.

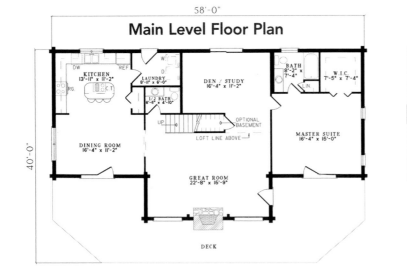

Main Level Floor Plan

Upper Level Floor Plan

Copyright by designer/architect.

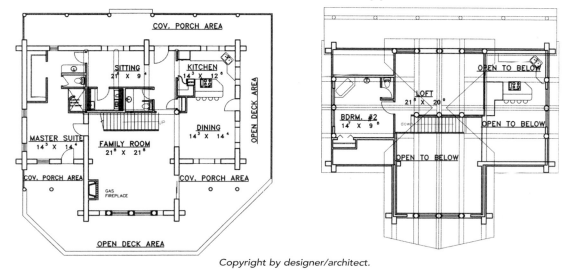

Plan #451036

Dimensions: 52' W x 60'2" D
Levels: 2
Square Footage: 2,576
Main Level Sq. Ft.: 1,852
Upper Level Sq. Ft.: 724
Bedrooms: 2
Bathrooms: 2
Foundation: Crawl space
Material List Available: No
Price Category: E

Images provided by designer/architect.

This home is filled with the spacious areas often found in larger footprints.

Features:

- Family Room: Relax with company or spend a quiet evening in this large, two-story family room, with its beautiful windows and gas fireplace.
- Kitchen: Plentiful counter space, an eating bar, and a walk-in pantry will make this

kitchen a pleasure to be in. A door leads out to the open deck and covered porch area, making meals outside easy.

- Master Suite: Located off the family room, this master suite features a large bedroom area and walk-in closet.
- Secondary Bedroom: Upstairs, a bedroom suite is perfect for an overnight guest or older child.

Main Level Floor Plan

COV. PORCH AREA

SITTING
21' X 9'

KITCHEN
14³ X 12⁸

OPEN DECK AREA

MASTER SUITE
14³ X 14⁴

FAMILY ROOM
21⁸ X 21⁸

DINING
14³ X 14⁴

COV. PORCH AREA

COV. PORCH AREA

GAS FIREPLACE

OPEN DECK AREA

Upper Level Floor Plan

OPEN TO BELOW

LOFT
21⁸ X 20⁹

BDRM. #2
14³ X 9⁸

OPEN TO BELOW

OPEN TO BELOW

Copyright by designer/architect.

Plan #451032

Dimensions: 66' W x 44'11" D
Levels: 2
Square Footage: 2,616
Main Level Sq. Ft.: 1,895
Upper Level Sq. Ft.: 721
Bedrooms: 3
Bathrooms: 2
Foundation: Walk out
Material List Available: No
Price Category: F

A large deck area spans the entire back of this home, wonderful for relaxing or entertaining guests.

Features:

- Mud Room: Conveniently located off the entry porch, this mud room is a great place to keep shoes, backpacks, or a drop zone for the family necessities.
- Kitchen: This beautiful kitchen features a two-story ceiling, a snack bar, and center workspace, and open access to the dining room, making entertaining easy.
- Great Room: You and your guests can relax in this two-story great room, with its access to the rear deck and beautiful window views.
- Master Suite: Upstairs, this master suite is secluded for privacy. The large bedroom area opens up to a bath featuring two walk-in closets, dual sinks, and a relaxing corner tub.

Main Level Floor Plan

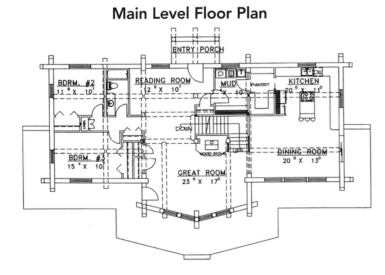

Upper Level Floor Plan

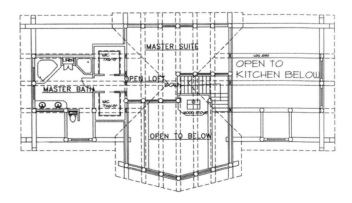

Plan #151758

Dimensions: 40' W x 36' D
Levels: 1.5
Square Footage: 1,725
Main Level Sq. Ft.: 1,120
Upper Level Sq. Ft.: 605
Bedrooms: 3
Bathrooms: 2
Foundation: Crawl space or basement; walk out for fee
Complete Cost List Available: Yes
Price Category: C

Images provided by designer/architect.

Here, you have found a traditional log home plan with a full covered porch and a simple yet refined floor plan.

Features:

Living Room: As you enter the home from the covered porch, this gathering area welcomes you. Feel the heat coming from the fireplace as you shake off the cold.

Kitchen: This peninsula kitchen is open to the dining room and the living room, giving the feeling of one open space. Step out the back door, and you can enjoy the great outdoors.

Bedrooms: Two bedrooms are located on the main level and share the main bathroom, which is located close by. The hallway closet, which holds the washer and dryer, is just a few steps away.

Upper Level: Up the L-shaped stairs brings you to the loft with an overview of the living room below. Bedroom 3 and the second full bathroom are also located on this level.

Main Level Floor Plan

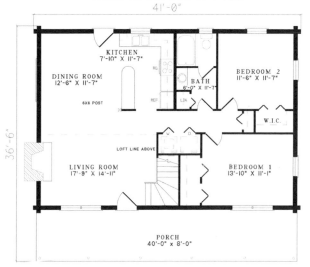

Upper Level Floor Plan

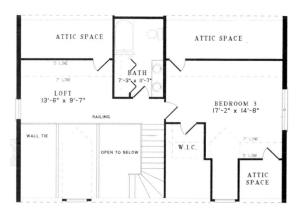

Copyright by designer/architect.

209

Plan #451037

Dimensions: 48'10" W x 77'7" D

Levels: 2

Square Footage: 2,532

Main Level Sq. Ft.: 1,273

Upper Level Sq. Ft.: 1,259

Bedrooms: 3

Bathrooms: 3

Foundation: Walk out

Material List Available: No

Price Category: E

This home features areas of open space, wonderful for decorating and utilizing as you please.

Features:

- Covered Deck Area: Surrounding the perimeter of the home, this deck is great when company arrives or when you want to simply sit back and enjoy the view.
- Kitchen: This large kitchen and dining area is spacious and open, wonderful when guests and family gather around this central hub of the home. An angled eating bar is perfect for grabbing a quick snack or chatting.
- Living Room: Adjacent to the kitchen, this living room features a large fireplace and beautiful views of the deck area.
- Master Suite: Upstairs, this master suite is isolated for privacy. The spacious bedroom area opens to a walk-in closet and a bathroom featuring a spa tub.

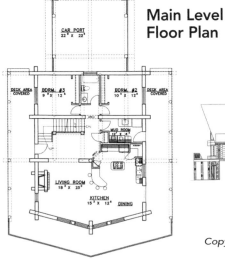

Main Level Floor Plan

Side Elevation

Upper Level Floor Plan

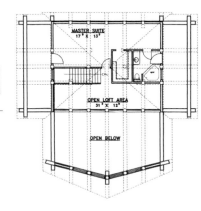

Lower Level Floor Plan

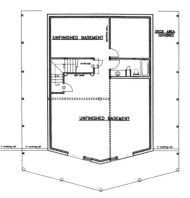

order direct: 1-800-523-6789

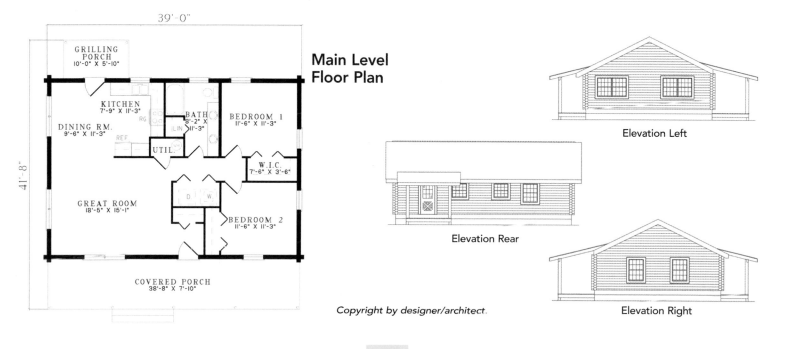

Plan #151761

Dimensions: 39' W x 41'8" D
Levels: 1
Square Footage: 1,092
Bedrooms: 2
Bathrooms: 1
Foundation: Crawl space
CompleteCost List Available: Yes
Price Category: B

Images provided by designer/architect.

This beautiful home is a simple straight-lined design featuring a front covered porch perfect for stargazing or enjoying a cup of hot chocolate.

Features:

• Kitchen: The L-shaped Kitchen has an angled island serving as extra counter space and additional seating. Nearby is a corner grilling porch with columns for lazy summer afternoons.

• Great Room: This large great room is airy and open to the dining room and kitchen, wonderful for entertaining or relaxing.

• Second Floor: The upper level has a spacious master suite, two additional bedrooms, a full bathroom and nearby laundry room.

**Main Level
Floor Plan**

39'-0"

GRILLING PORCH
10'-0" X 5'-10"

KITCHEN
7'-9" X 11'-3"

DINING RM.
9'-6" X 11'-3"

BATH
8'-2" X 11'-3"

REF

UTIL.

BEDROOM 1
11'-6" X 11'-3"

W.I.C.
7'-6" X 3'-6"

GREAT ROOM
18'-5" X 15'-1"

BEDROOM 2
11'-6" X 11'-3"

41'-8"

COVERED PORCH
38'-8" X 7'-10"

Elevation Left

Elevation Rear

Elevation Right

Copyright by designer/architect.

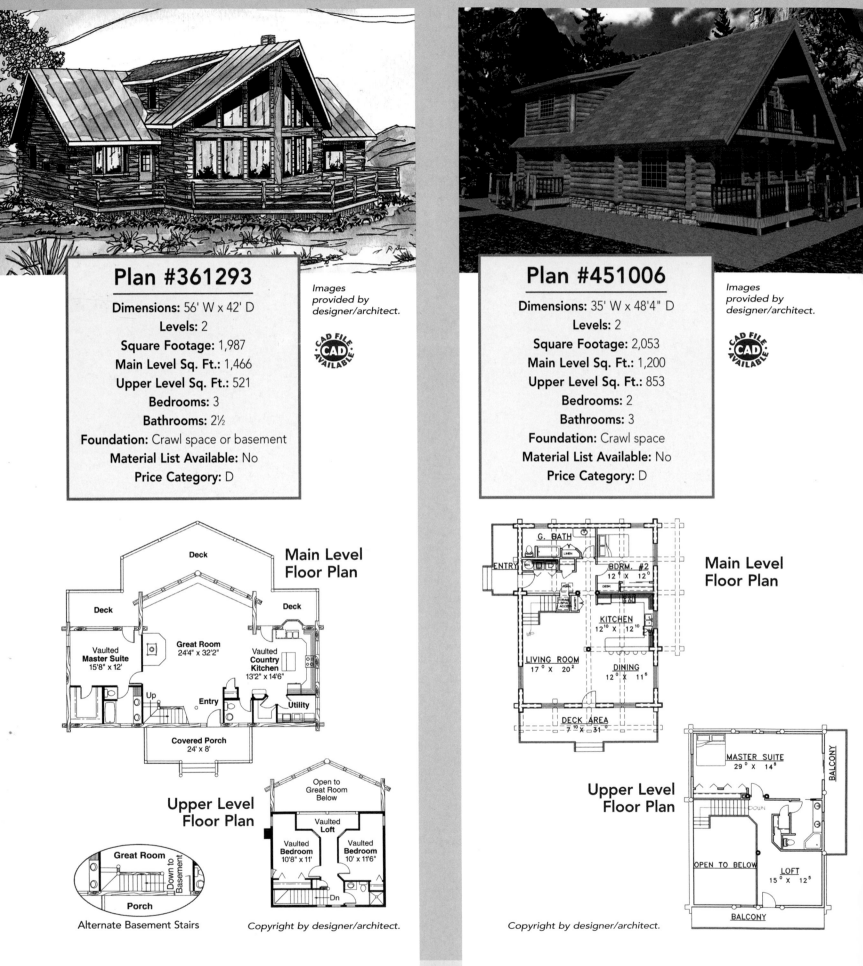

Plan #361293

Images provided by designer/architect.

Dimensions: 56' W x 42' D
Levels: 2
Square Footage: 1,987
Main Level Sq. Ft.: 1,466
Upper Level Sq. Ft.: 521
Bedrooms: 3
Bathrooms: 2½
Foundation: Crawl space or basement
Material List Available: No
Price Category: D

Main Level Floor Plan

Deck

Deck

Deck

Vaulted **Master Suite** 15'8" x 12'

Great Room 24'4" x 32'2"

Vaulted **Country Kitchen** 13'2" x 14'6"

Up

Entry

Utility

Covered Porch 24' x 8'

Upper Level Floor Plan

Open to Great Room Below

Vaulted **Loft**

Vaulted **Bedroom** 10'8" x 11'

Vaulted **Bedroom** 10' x 11'6"

Dn

Great Room

Down to Basement

Porch

Alternate Basement Stairs

Copyright by designer/architect.

Plan #451006

Images provided by designer/architect.

Dimensions: 35' W x 48'4" D
Levels: 2
Square Footage: 2,053
Main Level Sq. Ft.: 1,200
Upper Level Sq. Ft.: 853
Bedrooms: 2
Bathrooms: 3
Foundation: Crawl space
Material List Available: No
Price Category: D

Main Level Floor Plan

G. BATH

ENTRY

BDRM. #2 12'1" x 12'

KITCHEN 12'10 x 12'10

LIVING ROOM 17'0 X 20'2

DINING 12'0 X 11'6

DECK AREA 7'10 X 31'

Upper Level Floor Plan

MASTER SUITE 29'0 X 14'8

BALCONY

OPEN TO BELOW

LOFT 15'0 X 12'5

BALCONY

Copyright by designer/architect.

Plan #451026

Dimensions: 57' W x 56'8 D

Levels: 2

Square Footage: 2,577

Main Level Sq. Ft.: 1,500

Upper Level Sq. Ft.: 1,077

Bedrooms: 2

Bathrooms: 2½

Foundation: Slab

Material List Available: No

Price Category: E

Images provided by designer/architect.

CAD FILE **CAD** AVAILABLE

Main Level Floor Plan

Side Elevation

Lower Level Floor Plan

Upper Level Floor Plan

Copyright by designer/architect.

Plan #151756

Dimensions: 54' W x 52' D

Levels: 1.5

Square Footage: 2,137

Main Level Sq. Ft.: 1,556

Upper Level Sq. Ft.: 581

Bedrooms: 3

Bathrooms: 2½

Foundation: Crawl space; basement or walk out for fee

CompleteCost List Available: Yes

Price Category: D

Images provided by designer/architect.

Main Level Floor Plan

Upper Level Floor Plan

Copyright by designer/architect.

213

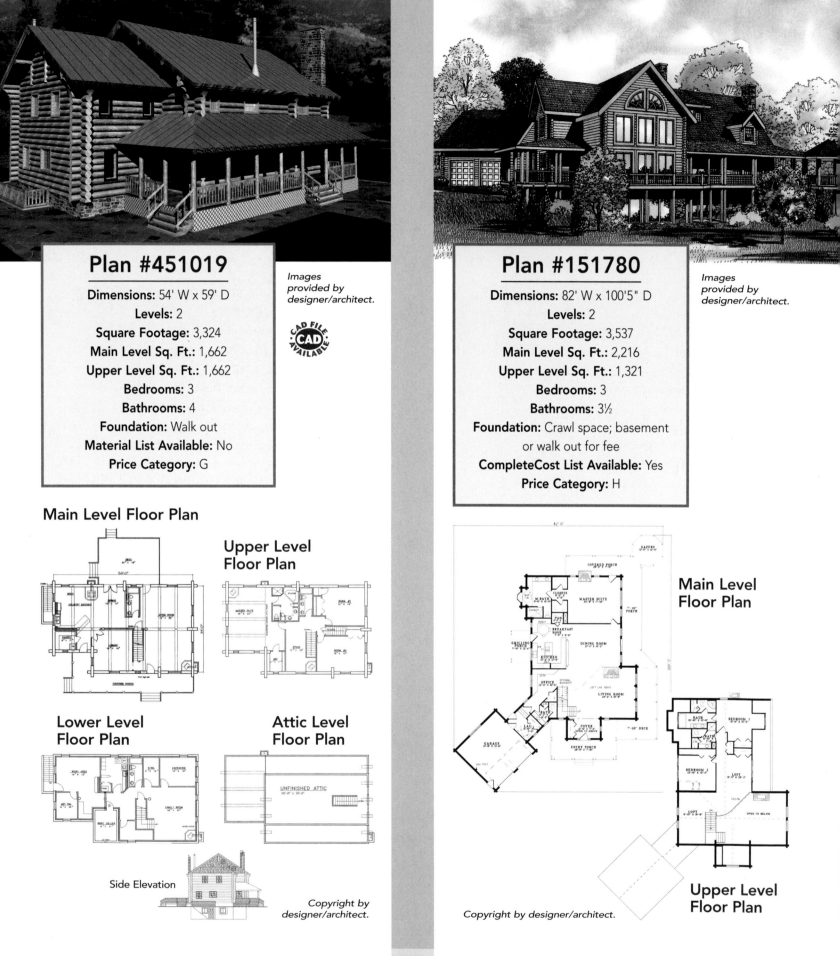

Plan #451019

Dimensions: 54' W x 59' D

Levels: 2

Square Footage: 3,324

Main Level Sq. Ft.: 1,662

Upper Level Sq. Ft.: 1,662

Bedrooms: 3

Bathrooms: 4

Foundation: Walk out

Material List Available: No

Price Category: G

Images provided by designer/architect.

CAD FILE AVAILABLE

Main Level Floor Plan

Upper Level Floor Plan

Lower Level Floor Plan

Attic Level Floor Plan

UNFINISHED ATTIC

Side Elevation

Copyright by designer/architect.

Plan #151780

Dimensions: 82' W x 100'5" D

Levels: 2

Square Footage: 3,537

Main Level Sq. Ft.: 2,216

Upper Level Sq. Ft.: 1,321

Bedrooms: 3

Bathrooms: 3½

Foundation: Crawl space; basement or walk out for fee

CompleteCost List Available: Yes

Price Category: H

Images provided by designer/architect.

Main Level Floor Plan

Upper Level Floor Plan

Copyright by designer/architect.

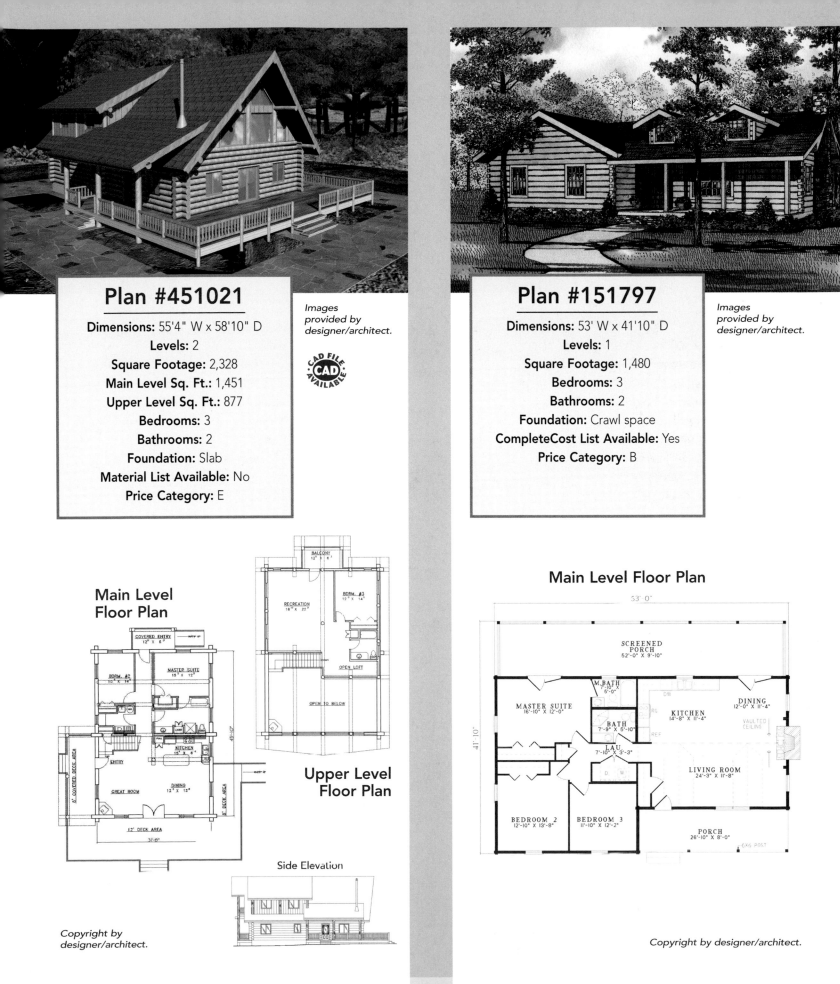

Plan #451021

Dimensions: 55'4" W x 58'10" D

Levels: 2

Square Footage: 2,328

Main Level Sq. Ft.: 1,451

Upper Level Sq. Ft.: 877

Bedrooms: 3

Bathrooms: 2

Foundation: Slab

Material List Available: No

Price Category: E

Images provided by designer/architect.

CAD FILE CAD AVAILABLE

Plan #151797

Dimensions: 53' W x 41'10" D

Levels: 1

Square Footage: 1,480

Bedrooms: 3

Bathrooms: 2

Foundation: Crawl space

CompleteCost List Available: Yes

Price Category: B

Images provided by designer/architect.

Main Level Floor Plan

Upper Level Floor Plan

Main Level Floor Plan

Side Elevation

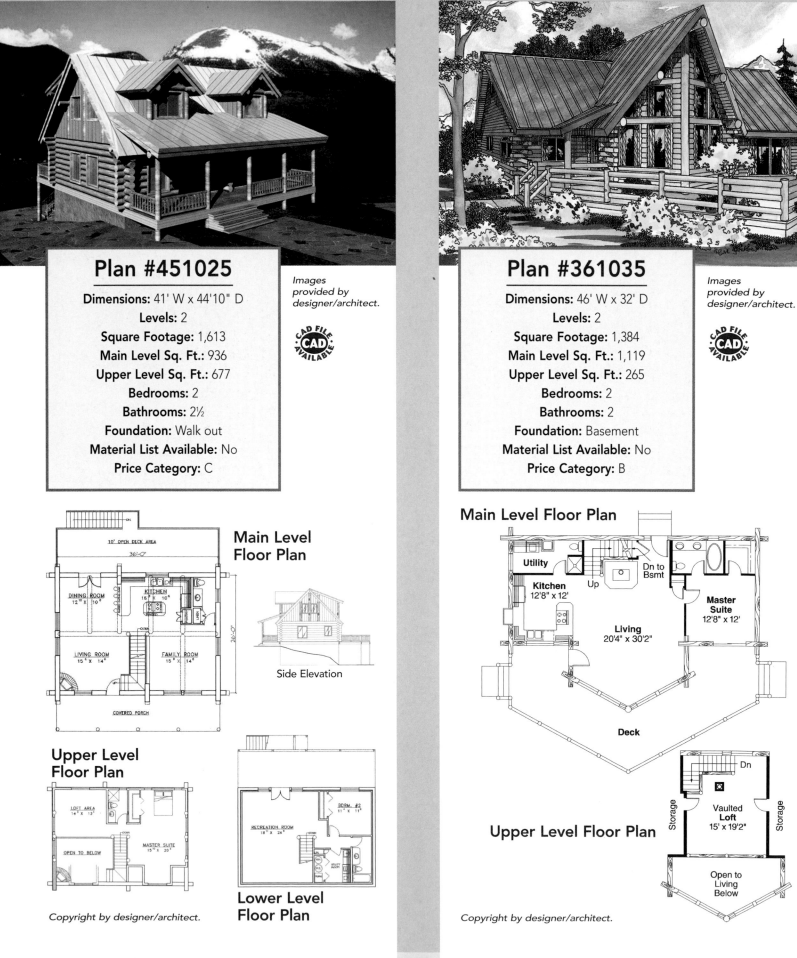

Plan #451025

Dimensions: 41' W x 44'10" D

Levels: 2

Square Footage: 1,613

Main Level Sq. Ft.: 936

Upper Level Sq. Ft.: 677

Bedrooms: 2

Bathrooms: 2½

Foundation: Walk out

Material List Available: No

Price Category: C

Images provided by designer/architect.

CAD FILE AVAILABLE

Main Level Floor Plan

Side Elevation

Upper Level Floor Plan

Lower Level Floor Plan

Copyright by designer/architect.

Plan #361035

Dimensions: 46' W x 32' D

Levels: 2

Square Footage: 1,384

Main Level Sq. Ft.: 1,119

Upper Level Sq. Ft.: 265

Bedrooms: 2

Bathrooms: 2

Foundation: Basement

Material List Available: No

Price Category: B

Images provided by designer/architect.

CAD FILE AVAILABLE

Main Level Floor Plan

Upper Level Floor Plan

Copyright by designer/architect.

216

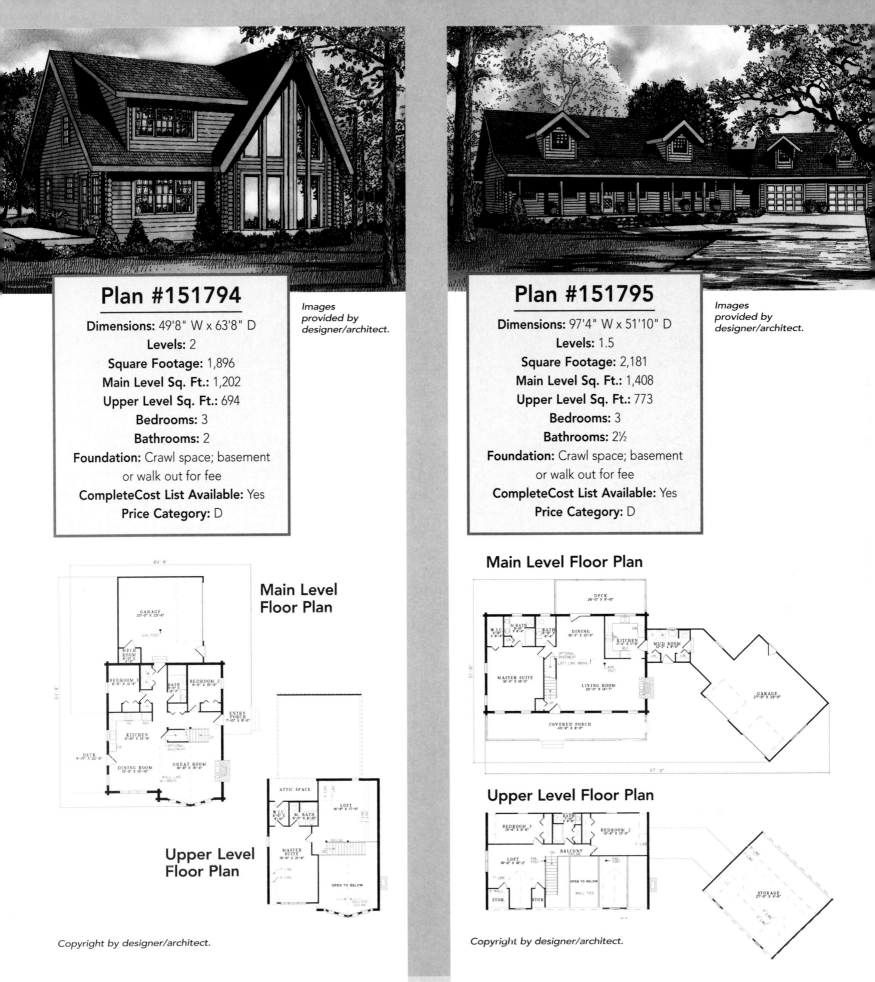

Plan #151794

Images provided by designer/architect.

Dimensions: 49'8" W x 63'8" D

Levels: 2

Square Footage: 1,896

Main Level Sq. Ft.: 1,202

Upper Level Sq. Ft.: 694

Bedrooms: 3

Bathrooms: 2

Foundation: Crawl space; basement or walk out for fee

CompleteCost List Available: Yes

Price Category: D

Main Level Floor Plan

Upper Level Floor Plan

Plan #151795

Images provided by designer/architect.

Dimensions: 97'4" W x 51'10" D

Levels: 1.5

Square Footage: 2,181

Main Level Sq. Ft.: 1,408

Upper Level Sq. Ft.: 773

Bedrooms: 3

Bathrooms: 2½

Foundation: Crawl space; basement or walk out for fee

CompleteCost List Available: Yes

Price Category: D

Main Level Floor Plan

Upper Level Floor Plan

Copyright by designer/architect.

Copyright by designer/architect.

Plan #151801

Dimensions: 45'8" W x 41'8" D

Levels: 1.5

Square Footage: 1,658

Main Level Sq. Ft.: 1,002

Upper Level Sq. Ft.: 656

Bedrooms: 3

Bathrooms: 2

Foundation: Crawl space; basement or walk out for fee

CompleteCost List Available: Yes

Price Category: C

Images provided by designer/architect.

This timeless log home is not only a complete design for a family but a work of art.

Features:

- **Living Room:** Vaulted ceilings of log beams gently weave the family areas together. This open living room is wonderful for entertaining, as guests can flow between the dining room and living room, and out onto the deck.
- **Kitchen:** Centrally located, this kitchen is complete with a center island workstation. An eating bar makes a quick snack or a relaxing cup of coffee even easier.
- **Master Suite:** You'll love to spend time in this beautiful master suite, with its walk-in closet, bath with double vanities, and private access to the deck outside.
- **Additional Bedrooms:** Both additional bedrooms each have a quaint dormer window and a private deck for late night stargazing.

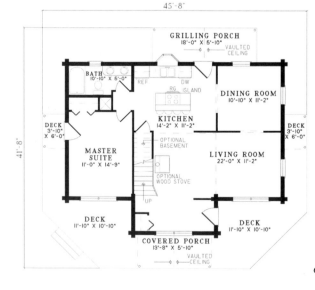

Main Level Floor Plan

Upper Level Floor Plan

Copyright by designer/architect.

Plan #451040

Dimensions: 32'6" W x 40'6" D
Levels: 2
Square Footage: 1,227
Main Level Sq. Ft.: 795
Upper Level Sq. Ft.: 432
Bedrooms: 3
Bathrooms: 3
Foundation: Walk out
Material List Available: No
Price Category: B

Images provided by designer/architect.

This home is both attractive and functional, perfect for all of your everyday needs.
Features:
- **Kitchen:** This kitchen area is large enough for multiple helping hands. An eating bar features seating for five, great for after-school snacks or help with dinner.
- **Living Room:** This living room will be great for entertaining your guests and family, and even opens up to the deck outside for additional space for entertaining in warm weather.
- **Master Suite:** Enter your personal oasis in this second-level master suite, which includes a patio, two vanities, and a walk-in closet.
- **Secondary Bedrooms:** Downstairs, two additional bedrooms are perfect for siblings, with walk-in closets and a shared bath.

Main Level Floor Plan

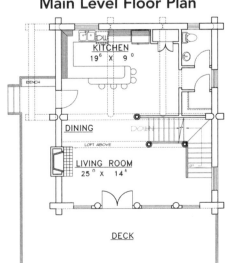

Upper Level Floor Plan

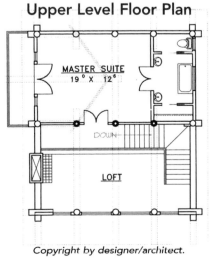

Copyright by designer/architect.

Lower Level Floor Plan

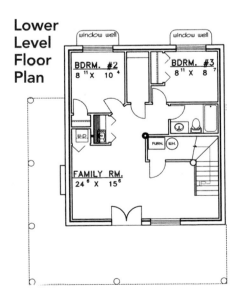

219

Plan #151768

Dimensions: 35' W x 39' D

Levels: 1.5

Square Footage: 1,122

Main Level Sq. Ft.: 775

Upper Level Sq. Ft.: 347

Bedrooms: 3

Bathrooms: 2

Foundation: Crawl space or basement; walk out for fee

CompleteCost List Available: Yes

Price Category: B

From the covered porch to the screened side porch, this log home was designed for comfort and convenience.

Features:

• Living Room: This room with corner fireplace has access to the screened porch and opens to the kitchen/dining area.

• Kitchen: This L-shaped kitchen is open to the living room and is located just off the entry.

• Master Suite: Upstairs you'll find this suite, with its large closet and private bath with double vanities.

• Bedrooms: The two secondary bedrooms, which share a common bathroom, are located on the main level and have ample closet space.

Main Level Floor Plan

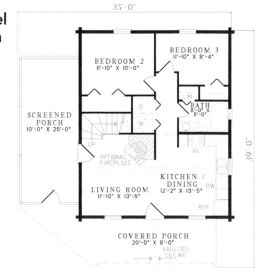

Upper Level Floor Plan

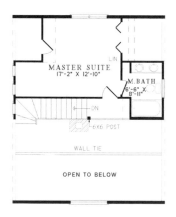

Plan #451044

Dimensions: 67'6" W x 69' D
Levels: 2
Square Footage: 3,219
Main Level Sq. Ft.: 2,089
Upper Level Sq. Ft.: 1,130
Bedrooms: 3
Bathrooms: 3½
Foundation: Crawl space
Material List Available: No
Price Category: G

Images provided by designer/architect.

If you love interesting architecture and uniquely shaped rooms, this home is perfect for you.

Features:

• Great Room: This beautiful spacious two-story great room angles out to the deck area and includes a fireplace, making it a wonderful space to entertain guests.

• Kitchen: Located directly off of the foyer, this kitchen is spacious enough for the home chef and little helping hands.

• Master Suite: This main-level master suite features access to the rear deck area, a tub, a walk-in closet, and a dual vanity.

• Deck Area: A large angled deck area envelops the rear of the home, perfect for meals outside or outdoor entertaining.

Main Level Floor Plan

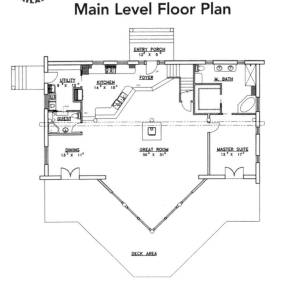

Upper Level Floor Plan

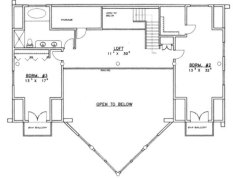

Rear Elevation

Copyright by designer/architect.

Plan #151778

Dimensions: 44' W x 45' D
Levels: 1.5
Square Footage: 1,810
Main Level Sq. Ft.: 1,276
Upper Level Sq. Ft.: 534
Bedrooms: 3
Bathrooms: 2½
Foundation: Crawl space
CompleteCost List Available: Yes
Price Category: D

Just imagine watching a sunset on the charming front porch of this log home.
Features:
• Open Plan: This open floor plan allows viewing the great room fireplace from both the dining room and kitchen, adding to the true enjoyment of the authentic log design.
• Dining Room: French doors in this room lead to a grilling porch, which has a handy eating bar to use as a buffet.
• Master Suite: This suite is privately located on the main level and is complete with a soothing whirlpool tub.
• Loft Area: This upstairs area leads to two additional bedrooms with ample closet space and plenty of natural light.

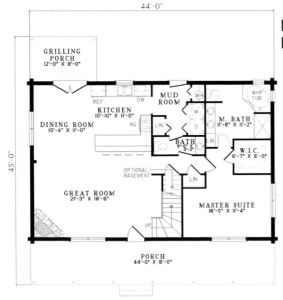

Main Level Floor Plan

Upper Level Floor Plan

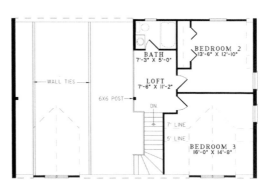

Plan #451049

Dimensions: 46'9" W x 29'7" D
Levels: 2
Square Footage: 2,263
Main Level Sq. Ft.: 1,412
Upper Level Sq. Ft.: 851
Bedrooms: 4
Bathrooms: 3
Foundation: Walk out
Material List Available: No
Price Category: E

Images provided by designer/architect.

This home features numerous amenities that you will love.

Features:

• Kitchen: This open and airy kitchen design is wonderful for the home cook, with a pantry area, center workspace, and adjacent dining nook. A door to the outside deck area makes outdoor meals easy.

• Master Suite: Upstairs, this large secluded master suite is complete with a walk-in closet, dual vanities, and a corner tub.

• Recreation Room: Downstairs, the recreation room is a great place for casual get-togethers.

• Mud Room: This room is perfect for keeping shoes and coats out of the rest of the home, in addition to storing those items that always seem to get left behind or lost before going out.

CAD FILE AVAILABLE

Main Level Floor Plan

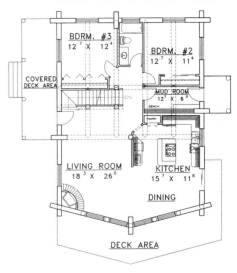

Upper Level Floor Plan

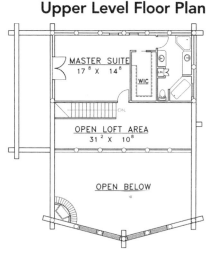

Lower Level Floor Plan

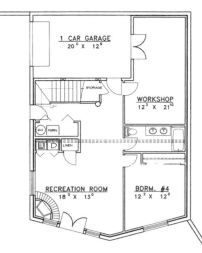

Copyright by designer/architect.

223

Plan #151789

Dimensions: 106'4" W x 57'8" D

Levels: 1.5

Square Footage: 2,521

Main Level Sq. Ft.: 1,645

Upper Level Sq. Ft.: 876

Bedrooms: 3

Bathrooms: 2

Foundation: Crawl space

CompleteCost List Available: Yes

Price Category: E

Images provided by designer/architect.

The full window view adds elegance to this log home, with its covered porches in the front and rear.

Features:

• Living Room: This room with fireplace has soaring vaulted ceiling and is open to the kitchen and dining room.

• Dining Room: To the right of the living room is this formal room, which opens to the kitchen with eating bar and has access to the laundry room and breezeway to the garage.

• Master Suite: This suite includes a walk-in closet and private bath, as well as access to the covered porch.

• Upper Level: This upper floor contains a loft and full bathroom between two bedrooms with ample closet space and access to the attic.

Main Level Floor Plan

Upper Level Floor Plan

Copyright by designer/architect.

Plan #451312

Dimensions: 46' W x 45' D
Levels: 2
Square Footage: 2,696
Main Level Sq. Ft.: 1,773
Upper Level Sq. Ft.: 923
Bedrooms: 1
Bathrooms: 2½
Foundation: Basement
Material List Available: No
Price Category: F

Images provided by designer/architect.

The covered decks on three sides of this home make a wonderful place to sit and relax or entertain.

Features:

• Kitchen: This kitchen is open to both the dining and great room on both sides, making it easy to transport dishes while entertaining.

• Master Suite: The large bedroom area opens up to a spacious walk-in closet and a roomy bathroom area featuring a dual vanity and corner tub.

• Office: Tucked away for privacy, this office is perfect for getting work done without being disturbed.

Main Level Floor Plan

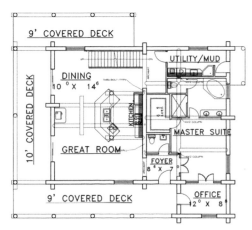

Upper Level Floor Plan

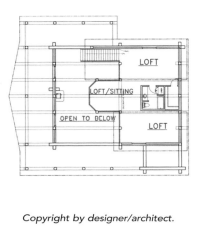

Copyright by designer/architect.

Lower Level Floor Plan

Side Elevation

Resource Guide

The following list of manufacturers and associations is meant to be a general guide to additional industry and product-related sources. It is not intended as a listing of products and manufacturers represented by the photographs in this book.

Amana
800-843-0304
www.amana.com
Manufactures refrigerators, dishwashers, and cooking appliances.

Antler Artistry
908-475-5974
www.antlerartistry.com
Manufactures lighting, furniture, and accessories made using antlers and natural processes.

Armstrong World Industries
717-397-0611
www.armstrong.com
Manufactures floors, cabinets, ceilings, and ceramic tiles.

Avalanche Ranch Light Company
888-841-1810
www.avalight.com
Manufactures handcrafted rustic lodge-style and Craftsman-style lighting.

Bach Faucets
866-863-6584
www.bachfaucet.com
Manufactures faucets.

Ballard Designs
800-536-7551
www.ballarddesigns.com
An online and catalog source for decorative accessories, including boxes and baskets.

Baltic Leisure
800-441-7147
www.balticleisure.com
Manufactures steam showers and saunas.

Bassett Furniture Industries
276-629-6000
www.bassettfurniture.com
Manufactures both upholstered furniture and casegoods.

Beaver Mountain Log & Cedar Homes
800-233-770
www.beavermtn.com
Manufactures custom-crafted log and cedar homes.

Blue Mountain Wallcoverings, Inc.
866-563-9872
www.imp-wall.com
Manufactures wallcoverings under the brand names Imperial, Sunworthy, Katzenbach & Warren, and Sanitas.

Bullock & Co.
705-424-5222
www.bullockloghomes.com
Builder and designers of custom handcrafted log homes, log cabins, and timber-frame homes.

Central Fireplace
800-248-4681
www.centralfireplace.com
Manufactures freestanding and zero-clearance fireplaces.

Cloudbird
509-997-2348
www.dancinglightlamps.com
Manufactures rustic lodge-style lighting.

Corian, a division of DuPont
800-426-7426
www.corian.com
Manufactures solid-surfacing material.

Comfortex Window Fashions
800-843-4151
www.comfortex.com
Manufactures custom window treatments, including sheer and pleated shades, wood shutters, and blinds. Its Web site provides company information and a store locator.

Country Curtains
800-456-0321
www.countrycurtains.com
A national retailer for ready-made curtains, shades, blinds, hardware, and accessories.

Custom Kitchen World, Inc.
845-735-5463
Distributes custom cabinetry.

**Crystal Farm Antler Chandeliers
and Furniture**
970-963-2350
www.crystalfarm.com
Manufactures rustic home furnishings and accessories.

Dex Studios
404-753-0600
www.dexstudios.com
Creates custom concrete sinks, tubs, and countertops.

Elkay
630-574-8484
www.elkayusa.com
Manufactures sinks, faucets, and countertops.

Elyria Fence Inc.
800-779-7581
www.elyriafence.com
*Provides custom fences, trellises, arbors, and decks
year-round. Its Web site has a photo gallery of its many
styles and designs.*

Expedition Log Homes
877-250-3300
www.expeditionloghomes.com
Manufactures custom handcrafted log homes.

Finnleo
800-346-6536
www.finnleo.com
Manufactures saunas, steam baths, and accessories.

Finn + Hattie, a division of Main Cottage
207-846-9166
www.finnandhattie.com
Manufactures juvenile furniture.

Frasier's Kitchen Showplace
715-365-3333
www.frasierskitchenshowplace.com
Specializes in kitchen and bath design.

Gandy/Peace Designs
404-237-8681
Specializes in interior design.

Garden Artisans
410-721-6185
www.gardenartisans.com
*Sells decorative backyard structures, such as garden art,
trellises, arbors, and planters, including a selection of
copper and metal structures.*

General Electric
580-634-0151
www.ge.com
Manufactures appliances and electronics.

Gone Wild Creations
716-699-6400
www.gonewildcreations.com
Manufactures rustic home furnishings and accessories.

The Great Camp Collection
970-963-0786
www.thegreatcampcollection.com
Manufactures ranch and lodge-style furniture.

Haier America
877-337-3639
www.haieramerica.com
*Manufactures electronics and appliances, including
wine cellars.*

Häfele America Co.
1-800-423-3531
www.hafeleonline.com
Manufactures cabinet hardware.

Hartco Hardwood Floors
800-769-8528
www.hartcoflooring.com
*Manufactures engineered hardwood and solid-wood
flooring.*

Hunter Douglas, Inc.
800-789-0331
www.hunterdouglas.com
Manufactures shades, blinds, and shutters.

Kohler
800-456-4537
www.kohler.com
Manufactures plumbing products.

Kraftmaid Cabinetry
440-632-5333
www.kraftmaid.com
Manufactures cabinetry.

LG
800-243-0000
www.lge.com
Manufactures major appliances.

Lightology
866-954-4489
www.lightology.com
Manufactures lighting fixtures.

Maine Cottage Furniture
888-859-5522
www.mainecottage.com
Manufactures casual home furnishings.

Maple Island Log Homes
1-800-748-0137
www.mapleisland.com
Manufactures handcrafted log homes.

Miller Architects, PC
406-222-7057
www.ctmarchitects.com
Designs custom log homes.

Midnight Farms
828-743-5858
www.midnightfarms.com
Manufactures rustic home furnishings and accessories.

Moen
800-289-6636
www.moen.com
Manufactures plumbing products.

Motif Design
800-431-2424
www.motif-designs.com
Manufactures furniture, fabrics, and wallcoverings.

New West
800-653-2391
www.newwest.com
Custom designs and manufactures Western-style furniture.

Old Hickory
800-232-2275
www.oldhickory.com
Manufactures ranch, cabin, and lodge-style furniture.

Osram-Sylvania
978-777-1900
www.sylvania.com
Manufactures lighting products and accessories.

Plaid Industries
800-842-4197
www.plaidonline.com
Manufactures stencils, stamps, and craft paints.

Plain and Fancy Custom Cabinetry
800-447-9006
www.plainfancycabinetry.com
Makes custom cabinetry.

Plow & Hearth
800-494-7544
www.plowhearth.com
A national catalog, retail, and Internet company specializing in home and lifestyle products.

Price Pfister, Inc.
800-732-8238
www.pricepfister.com
Manufactures faucets.

Quoizel
631-273-2700
www.quoizel.com
Manufactures lighting and home accessories.

Restoration Hardware
800-910-9836
www.restorationhardware.com
Sells indoor and outdoor furniture, windows, hardware, and lighting accessories.

Rustic Furniture
406-285-6882
www.rusticfurniture.net
Manufactures custom-designed furniture.

Santos Furniture
888-966-3489
www.santosfurniture.com
Designs and manufactures art furniture and Molesworth reproductions.

Southwest Door Company
520-574-7374
www.southwestdoor.com
Manufactures windows, doors, and flooring for log homes.

Springs Industries, Inc.
888-926-7888
www.springs.com
Manufactures window treatments, including blinds and shutters, and distributes Graber Hardware.

Stencil Ease
800-334-1776
www.stencilease.com
Manufactures laser-cut stencils and related tools and supplies.

Stickley
315-682-5500
www.stickley.com
Sells vintage-style and traditional furniture.

Tarkett
www.tarkett-floors.com
Manufactures vinyl, laminate, tile, and wood flooring.

Thibaut Inc.
800-223-0704
www.thibautdesign.com
Manufactures wallpaper and fabrics.

Viers Furniture Co.
406-222-7564
www.montanawesternfurn.com
Manufactures traditional, Western-style furniture.

Whirlpool Corp.
www.whirlpool.com
Manufactures home appliances and related products, including a drying cabinet and an ironing center.

Whispering Pines
203-259-5027
www.whisperingpinescatalog.com
Sells log-cabin-style accessories and home furnishings, including lighting and fabric.

Wood-Mode Fine Custom Cabinetry
877-635-7500
www.wood-mode.com
Manufactures custom cabinetry for the kitchen.

Yellowstone Traditions
406-587-0968
www.yellowstonetraditions.com
Manufactures custom homes.

York Wallcoverings
717-846-4456
www.yorkwall.com
Manufactures borders and wallcoverings.

Glossary

Accent Lighting: A type of lighting that highlights an area or object to emphasize that aspect of a room's character.

Accessible Designs: Those that accommodate persons with physical disabilities.

Adaptable Designs: Those that can be easily changed to accommodate a person with disabilities.

Analogous Scheme: See Harmonious Color Scheme.

Ambient Lighting: General illumination that surrounds a room. There is no visible source of the light.

Arts and Crafts Movement: A decorative style that began in England during the late nineteenth century, where it was known as the Aesthetic Movement. Lead by William Morris, the movement rejected industrialization and encouraged fine craftsmanship and simplicity in design.

Backlighting: Illumination coming from a source behind or at the side of an object.

Backsplash: The vertical part at the rear and sides of a countertop that protects the adjacent wall.

Box Pleat: A double pleat, underneath which the edges fold toward each other.

Broadloom: A wide loom for weaving carpeting that is 54 inches wide or more.

Built-In: Any element, such as a bookcase or cabinetry, that is built into a wall or an existing frame.

Cabriole: A double-curve or reverse S-shaped furniture leg that leads down to an elaborate foot (usually a ball-and-claw type).

Candlepower: The luminous intensity of a beam of light (total luminous flux) in a particular direction, measured in units called candelas.

Casegoods: A piece of furniture used for storage, including cabinets, dressers, and desks.

Clearance: The amount of space between two fixtures, the centerlines of two fixtures, or a fixture and an obstacle, such as a wall.

Code: A locally or nationally enforced mandate regarding structural design, materials, plumbing, or electrical systems that state what you can or cannot do when you build or remodel.

Color Wheel: A pie-shaped diagram showing the range and relationships of pigment and dye colors.

Complementary Colors: Hues directly opposite each other on the color wheel. As the strongest contrasts, complements tend to intensify each other.

Contemporary: Any modern design (after 1920) that does not contain traditional elements.

Cove: 1. A built-in recess in a wall or ceiling that conceals an indirect light source. 2. A concave recessed molding that is usually found where the wall meets the ceiling or floor.

Daybed: A bed made up to appear as a sofa. It usually has a frame that consists of a headboard, a footboard, and a sideboard along the back.

Dimmer Switch: A switch that can vary the intensity of the light it controls.

Distressed Finish: A decorative paint technique in which the final paint coat is sanded and battered to produce an aged appearance.

Dovetail: A joinery method in which wedge-shaped parts are interlocked to form a tight bond. This joint is commonly used in furniture making.

Dowel: A short cylinder, made of wood, metal, or plastic, that fits into corresponding holes bored in two pieces of wood, creating a joint.

Faux Finish: A decorative paint technique that imitates a pattern found in nature.

Federal: An architectural and decorative style popular in America during the early nineteenth century, featuring delicate ornamentation and symmetrically arranged rooms.

Fittings: The plumbing devices that bring water to the fixtures, such as faucets.

Fluorescent Lighting: A glass tube coated on the interior with phosphor, a chemical compound that emits light when activated by ultraviolet energy. Air in the tube is replaced with a combination of argon gas and a small amount of mercury.

Focal Point: The dominant element in a room or design, usually the first to catch your eye.

Footcandle: A unit that is used to measure brightness. A footcandle is equal to one lumen per square foot of surface.

Framed Cabinet: A cabinet with a full frame across the face of the cabinet box.

Frameless Cabinet: A cabinet without a face frame. It may also be called a "European-style" cabinet.

Frieze: A horizontal band at the top of the wall or just below the cornice.

Full-Spectrum Light: Light that contains the full range of wavelengths that can be found in daylight, including invisible radiation at the end of each visible spectrum.

Gateleg Table: A drop-leaf table supported by a gate-like leg that folds or swings out.

Ground-Fault Circuit Interrupter (GFCI): A safety circuit breaker that compares the amount of current entering a receptacle with the amount leaving. If there is a discrepancy of 0.005 volt, the GFCI breaks the circuit in a fraction of a second. GFCIs are required in damp areas of the house.

Grout: A mortar that is used to fill the spaces between tiles.

Hardware: Wood, plastic, or metal-plated trim found on the exterior of furniture, such as knobs, handles, and decorative trim.

Harmonious Color Scheme: Also called analogous, a combination focused on neighboring hues on the color wheel. The shared underlying color generally gives such schemes a coherent flow.

Hue: Another term for specific points on the pure, clear range of the color wheel.

Incandescent Lighting: A bulb (lamp) that converts electric power into light by passing electric current through a filament of tungsten wire.

Indirect Lighting: A more subdued type of lighting that is not head-on, but rather reflected against another surface such as a ceiling.

Inlay: A decoration, usually consisting of stained wood, metal, or mother-of-pearl, that is set into the surface of an object in a pattern and finished flush.

Lambrequin: Drapery that hangs from a shelf, such as a mantel, or covering the top of a window or a door. This term is sometimes used interchangeably with valance.

Love Seat: A sofa-like piece of furniture that consists of seating for two.

Lumen: The measurement of a source's light output—the quantity of visible light.

Lumens Per Watt (LPW): The ratio of the amount of light provided to the energy (watts) used to produce the light.

Modular: Units of a standard size, such as pieces of a sofa, that can be fitted together.

Molding: An architectural band used to trim a line where materials join or create a linear decoration. It is typically made of wood, plaster, or a polymer.

Mortise-and-Tenon Joinery: A hole (mortise) cut into a piece of wood that receives a projecting piece (tenon) to create a joint.

Occasional Piece: A small piece of furniture for incidental use, such as end tables.

Orientation: The placement of any object or space, such as a window, a door, or a room, and its relationship to the points on a compass.

Panel: A flat, rectangular piece of material that forms part of a wall, door, or cabinet. Typically

made of wood, it is usually framed by a border and either raised or recessed.

Parquet: Inlaid woodwork arranged to form a geometric pattern. It consists of small blocks of wood, which are often stained in contrasting colors.

Pattern Matching: To align a repeating pattern when joining together two pieces of fabric.

Pediment: A triangular piece found over doors, windows, and occasionally mantels. It also refers to a low-pitched gable on the front of a building.

Peninsula: A countertop, with or without a base cabinet, that is connected at one end to a wall or another counter and extends outward, providing access on three sides.

Primary Color: Red, blue, or yellow that can't be produced in pigments by mixing other colors. Primaries plus black and white, in turn, combine to make all the other hues.

Secondary Color: A mix of two primaries. The secondary colors are orange, green, and purple.

Sectional: Furniture made into separate pieces that coordinate with each other. The pieces can be arranged together as a large unit or independently.

Slipcover: A fabric or plastic cover that can be draped or tailored to fit over a piece of furniture.

Stud: A vertical support element made of wood or metal that is used in the construction of walls.

Task Lighting: Lighting that concentrates in specific areas for tasks, such as preparing food, applying makeup, reading, or doing crafts.

Tone: Degree of lightness or darkness of a color.

Tongue-and-Groove Joinery: A joinery technique in which a protruding end (tongue) fits into a recess (groove), locking the two pieces together.

Track Lighting: Lighting that utilizes a fixed band that supplies a current to movable light fixtures.

Trompe L'oeil: Literally meaning "fool the eye," a painted mural in which realistic images and the illusion of more space are created.

Tufting: The fabric of an upholstered piece or a mattress that is drawn tightly to secure the padding, creating regularly spaced indentations.

Turning: Wood that is cut on a lathe into a round object with a distinctive profile. Furniture legs or posts are usually made in this way.

Uplight: Also used to describe the lights themselves, this is actually the term for light that is directed upward toward the ceiling.

Valance: Short drapery that hangs along the top of a window, with or without a curtain underneath.

Value: In relation to a scale of grays ranging from black to white, this is the term to describe the lightness (tints) or darkness (shades) of a color.

Veneer: High-quality wood that is cut into very thin sheets for use as a surface material.

Wainscotting: A wallcovering of boards, plywood, or paneling that covers the lower section of an interior wall and usually contrasts with the wall surface above.

Welt: A cord, often covered by fabric, that is used as an elegant trim on cushions, slipcovers, and pillows.

Work Triangle: The area bounded by the lines that connect the sink, range, and refrigerator. A kitchen may have multiple work triangles. In an ideal triangle, the distances between appliances are from 4 to 9 feet.

Index

Photo Credits

pages 1–7: Roger Wade **page 8:** *left* Jack Bingham Studio; right Roger Wade **page 9:** Roger Wade **pages 10–11:** *both* Jack Bingham Studio **page 13:** Daniel Newcomb **pages 14–17:** *all* courtesy of Rocky Home Mountain Log Homes **pages 18–33:** *all* Jack Bingham Studio **pages 34–39:** *all* Roger Wade **page 40:** Tria Giovan **pages 41–46:** *all* Roger Wade **page 47:** courtesy of Rocky Home Mountain Log Homes **page 48:** Roger Wade **page 49:** *left* Roger Wade; *right* Tria Giovan **page 50:** Roger Wade **page 52:** Rob Karosis **page 53:** Roger Wade **page 54:** *left* Roger Wade; *right* Rob Karosis **page 55:** *top* Olson Photographic, LLC; *bottom* Jack Bingham Studio **pages 56–58:** *all* Roger Wade **page 59:** Mark Lohman **pages 60–61:** *both* Roger Wade **pages 63–76**: *all* Roger Wade **page 77:** Olson Photographic, LLC **pages 78–93:** *all* Roger Wade **page 94:** *top and bottom left* Roger Wade; *bottom right* Robin Stubbert **pages**

95–100: *all* Roger Wade **page 101:** *top* Jack Bingham Studio; *bottom* Roger Wade **page 102–104:** *all* Roger Wade **page 105:** *top* Roger Wade; *bottom* Jack Bingham Studio **page 106:** Jack Bingham Studio **page 107:** Tria Giovan **page 108:** Rob Karosis **page 109:** Roger Wade **page 110:** Jack Bingham Studio **pages 112–114:** *all* Roger Wade **page 115:** Mark Lohman **page 116:** Roger Wade **page 118:** *top* courtesy of Rocky Mountain Log Homes; *bottom* Roger Wade **page 119:** Mark Lohman **pages 120–121:** *both* Roger Wade **page 122:** *top* Jack Bingham Studio; *bottom* Roger Wade **page 123:** Jack Bingham Studio **pages 124–127:** *all* Roger Wade **page 128:** Jack Bingham Studio **page 129:** Roger Wade **pages 130–131:** *both* Jack Bingham Studio **pages 132–133:** *both* Tria Giovan **pages 134–135:** *both* Jack Bingham Studio **pages 136–193:** *all* Roger Wade

If **Dream Log Homes & Plans** has inspired you, look for these other idea-packed books from **Creative Homeowner** wherever books are sold.

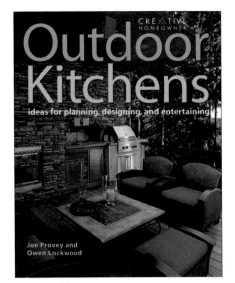

Outdoor Kitchens showcases fully equipped year-round designs for every budget and any part of the country.

Over 320 photographs. 224 pp.
$21.95 (US) $23.95 (CAN)
BOOK #: 277571

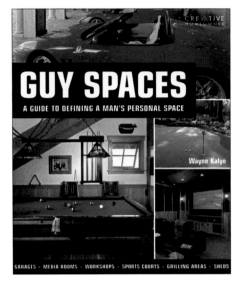

Guy Spaces addresses those areas in and around the house that are traditionally for guys only—garages, media and game rooms, grilling spaces, and more. *Paperback.*

Over 250 photographs. 208 pp.
$19.95 (US) $21.95 (CAN)
BOOK #: 279529

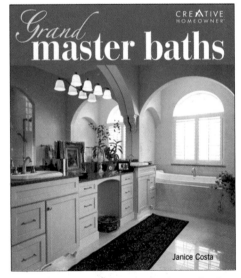

Grand Master Baths is a stunning collection of the latest design ideas and solutions for creating a beautiful, restful, and highly functional master-bath escape.

Over 300 photographs. 208 pp.
$19.95 (US) $21.95 (CAN)
BOOK #: 279044

Design Ideas for Home Decorating is a general decorating book that presents design solutions for every room in the house, and for every budget. *Paper with flaps.*

Over 500 photographs. 320 pp.
$19.95 (US) $24.95 (CAN)
BOOK #: 279323

For more information on our HOME IMPROVEMENT, DECORATING, LANDSCAPING, and HOME ARTS books, visit **www.creativehomeowner.com**.